"*The Chinese Exodus* is a moving descri[ption based on] research and extensive personal intervie[ws of the uprooting] and destruction of social bonds experie[nced by those mi-]grated from the rural areas of China to [cities. Li Ma describes] that, and it's the 'more' that makes Li M[a's book especially] important. She interweaves her descriptions of urban poverty and social disorientation in China with a rich and passionate Christian theological interpretation of those phenomena."

—**Nicholas Wolterstorff**, Noah Porter Professor Emeritus of Philosophical Theology, Yale University

"This profoundly important book provides an in-depth study of one of the major crises in contemporary China: the tragic plight of the large numbers of rural poor who have migrated to urban centers in recent years. These folks experience difficult—indeed, in many cases, unspeakable—hardships. Li Ma not only describes the contours of their lives with impressive sociological insight, but she also advocates on their behalf by making it clear that their plight touches the very heart of God. I hope that this fine book moves many human hearts—as it has moved mine!"

—**Richard Mouw**, President Emeritus and Professor of Faith and Public Life, Fuller Theological Seminary

"This book ... exposes the unbearable burden upon millions and millions of rural migrants ... in the former communist countries whose population lived mostly in the countryside at the time of their opening and reform. Li Ma ... goes beyond the 'scientific research' of the phenomena. Poverty, deprivation, and alienation can be described and analyzed, but she points out convincingly that the root lies deeper. Only with faith in God can migrants get internal freedom and the sense of being equal before God."

—**Jingbei Hu**, Professor Emeritus of Economics, Tongji University

"In the past two decades China has witnessed the most massive peacetime internal migration in the history of the world. Ma's groundbreaking study of China's urban migrants combines careful sociological research with deep theological reflection as she responds to the biblical injunction to both 'know the stranger' and 'welcome the stranger.' Her penetrating analysis reveals the paradox of those who, due to the entrenched discrimination of China's socialist system and the forces of capitalist domination, live as immigrants in their own country."

—**Brent Fulton**, President, ChinaSource

"What does it look like when a country with a history of class division mixes communism and capitalism? China and the plight of migrants cannot be understood without careful analysis, and this book provides multiple key insights by placing the story of urban migration, and the resulting effects on individuals, families, and children, within economic, sociological, and theological frameworks. The result is deep and profound understandings that help us see the suffering, and some of the pathways for coming alongside those who suffer injustice. It is a must resource for understanding China today."

—**Jul Medenblik**, President of Calvin Theological Seminary

"Li Ma captures voices of Chinese migrant workers that most of us would otherwise never hear. To the outside world China's material gains and economic power are the image of the nation. Li Ma presents the costs Chinese working people pay. Her voice challenges the god of money."

—**Thomas Post**, World Renew

"*The Chinese Exodus* offers a comprehensive and poignant account of Chinese migrant workers' struggle and survival under immense structural and cultural discriminations. Evoking prophetic imaginations, Dr. Ma masterfully weaves together sociological investigation, social theory, and theological insights to expose the deep injustice of the present and to plant a subversive hope for the future. She challenges us to dislodge our institutionalized prejudices and proactively and creatively work to redeem and restore what is broken and lost in our world."

—**Min-Dong Paul Lee**, Norris A. Aldeen Professor of Business, Wheaton College

The Chinese Exodus

The Chinese Exodus

Migration, Urbanism, and
Alienation in Contemporary China

LI MA

☙PICKWICK *Publications* • Eugene, Oregon

THE CHINESE EXODUS
Migration, Urbanism, and Alienation in Contemporary China

Copyright © 2018 Li Ma. All rights reserved. Except for brief quotations in critical publications or reviews, no part of this book may be reproduced in any manner without prior written permission from the publisher. Write: Permissions, Wipf and Stock Publishers, 199 W. 8th Ave., Suite 3, Eugene, OR 97401.

Pickwick Publications
An Imprint of Wipf and Stock Publishers
199 W. 8th Ave., Suite 3
Eugene, OR 97401

www.wipfandstock.com

PAPERBACK ISBN: 978-1-5326-4597-6
HARDCOVER ISBN: 978-1-5326-4598-3
EBOOK ISBN: 978-1-5326-4599-0

Cataloguing-in-Publication data:

Names: Ma, Li, author.

Title: The Chinese exodus : migration, urbanism, and alienation in contemporary China / Li Ma.

Description: Eugene, OR: Pickwick Publications, 2018. | Includes bibliographical references and index.

Identifiers: ISBN 978-1-5326-4597-6 (paperback). | ISBN 978-1-5326-4598-3 (hardcover). | ISBN 978-1-5326-4599-0 (ebook).

Subjects: LCSH: Theology, practical. | Emigration and immigration—Religious aspects—Christianity. | Social change—China. | Cities and towns—Religious aspects—Christianity. | Rural-urban migration—China. | China—History—1949-.

Classification: BV4647 H67 M25 2018 (print). | BV4647 (ebook).

Scripture taken from the New King James Version®. Copyright © 1982 by Thomas Nelson. Used by permission. All rights reserved.

Manufactured in the U.S.A.   06/29/18

For Jin Li

Contents

Acknowledgments | ix

1. Introduction | 1
2. The Regime and the Underclass | 12
3. Urbanism and Alienation | 36
4. The Loss of Community | 70
5. Good Samaritans | 97
6. Conclusion: Hope for a City | 115

Bibliography | 129
Index | 137

Acknowledgments

THE RESEARCH AND WRITING of this book took twelve years. My initial interest on China's internal migration and urban poverty was closely related to my family history. Rural-urban inequality is a part of Chinese reality that I grew up with. Later at Cornell University, I decided on it as my doctoral dissertation project. There I received cordial support from a world-class Weberian scholar Richard Swedberg and a China expert Victor Nee.

I am indebted to the Center for the Study of Economy and Society, the Center for the Study of Social Inequality, and the East Asian Program at Cornell University for a few research grants from 2006 to 2008 in support of my field research.

While doing this research, the insights of a few Chinese economists also contributed to my research: Jingbei Hu, Weisen Li, Xuncheng Du and Jin Li. Two other scholars in Shanghai also shared their views with me on this project: Xueqin Zhu and Xin Liu.

I also remember getting help and advice from Yingfang Chen at Shanghai Transportation University, Jingming Xiong at the Universities Service Center for China Studies at Hong Kong Chinese University. They both struck me as compassionate and conscientious senior scholars.

I appreciate the friendships of two scholars from Taiwan, Pei-Chia Lan and Jieh-Min Wu, who were also doing research on the same topic of migration and Chinese politics. It was encouraging for me to know that this problem was also close to their hearts.

I spent a few summers with NGO workers who later became dear friends, including Chuanmei Sun, Jianing and Lydia

Zhang, Yongchang Qian, and anthropologist Ziqi Ou at Columbia University.

My special appreciation is also extended to Brent Fulton, President of ChinaSource. Over the years, Dr. Fulton has been supportive of my efforts in extending sociological observation to theological discussions. I am also indebted to Joann Pittman who has generously let me use some photos she took in China.

Many other people have offered support during my writing. I first have to thank my husband Jin Li. He is the one who constantly encouraged and pushed me to finish this manuscript. A best companion in life, Jin has also brought major intellectual transformations in me. So it is to him that I dedicate this volume.

While living in Grand Rapids, Michigan, I was grateful for making the acquaintance of a distinguished scholar Nicolas Wolterstorff, and I benefited from his modeling of Christian conscience on issues of social justice. Corwin Smidt and Kevin den Dulk at the Henry Institute for the Study of Christianity and Politics at Calvin College have always offered encouragement. I am also especially grateful to Emily Brink for her careful reading of this manuscript. She offered helpful suggestions for improvement.

My thanks also go to Wright Doyle and Carol Hamrin of the Global China Center for their inspiring friendships. Dr. Grant Chen in California has also been supportive about my various attempts at integrating sociology and theology. I also appreciate the friendship of Dr. Keith Campbell of Global Scholars who keenly supported my interdisciplinary scholarship.

Many thanks to Harriette Mostert for her careful editing help.

Last but not least, my appreciation goes to the anonymous many, rural migrants and NGO workers, who shared with me their life stories.

Soli Deo Gloria

Li Ma
Grand Rapids, Michigan

1

Introduction

> Like slavery and apartheid, poverty is not natural.
> It is man-made.
>
> —Nelson Mandela

IN A DESERTED VILLAGE home within China's poorest countryside, Guizhou Province, after years of laboring to care for his three younger siblings, a fourteen-year-old boy named Ren left a suicide note. It said, "I made a vow that I wouldn't live past the age of fifteen. I am fourteen now. I dream about death, and yet that dream never comes true. Today it must finally come true." After writing the note, Ren poisoned his younger siblings and then himself.

This disturbing news in the summer of 2015 is just one of many tragic stories of the nation's systemic neglect of children "left behind" due to rural out-migration in recent years. Economic decadence in rural parts of China have forced their desperate residents to seek work in urban centers while leaving their children with grandparents or relatives in villages.[1] Media stories of sexual abuse suffered by rural school-aged children unattended by their parents have also become common.[2]

Some equally grueling stories about migrants come from urban China. For instance, fourteen migrant workers at the world's largest electronics factory, Foxconn, jumped off the tallest building

---

1. Ma, "China Raises," 214.
2. Between 2008 and 2011, Guangdong Province alone dealt with more than 1,700 cases. Quoted in Wu, "Abuse," para. 11; see "Sexual Abuse of Children."

to end their lives in 2010, followed by more deaths and hundreds of suicide protesters since then. Despite the Chinese government's claims to have eliminated abject poverty for one-fourth of the global population by leading a fast-growing economy, nevertheless poverty, death and abuse seem to linger closer than they did two decades ago, and often in more dramatic ways.

When the first snow fell in Beijing in November of 2017, the government launched a large-scale safety crackdown on illegal housing after a fire killed nineteen people.[3] In just forty hours, over three million migrant workers were evicted by force. Many were given only an hour's notice to leave, with mafia-like figures appearing at the door to enforce immediate evacuation. Many vibrant migrant-concentrated areas in Beijing suddenly became near-war-zones. Leftover daily necessities piled up, and homeless migrants slept on the roadside. News photos of demolished living zones with toys and unfinished instant food scattered about testified to how suddenly it happened.

When the state media coined a new word, "low-end population" (*diduan renkou*), in their policies, it incurred outcry on the Internet. Photos of homeless elderly migrants and a nursing mother in tears holding her infant while packing her belongings angered a stratum of affluent and educated residents of the capital, who protested such inhumane treatment of their own countrymen.[4] Two to three days after the event, some charity groups posted offers of rides and shelter online, but a few were immediately muted by the Internet police, warning of their "[violation of] regulations."[5]

Just like ancient Hebrew slaves in Egypt, rural migrants comprise the backbone of China's working force and economic boom. And, like slaves, they are also an acquiescent underclass suffering from both cruel market forces and the whims of communist policy-makers. Even though they sustain the urban economy, rural migrants remain a faceless, disposable group. Their presence is most visibly felt during the annual homecoming at the Lunar New

3. Dou and Fong, "Homeward Bound."
4. Zhuang, "Evictions Waken Beijing Middle Class."
5. Caiman, "In Beijing, a Mass Eviction," para. 14.

INTRODUCTION

Year, the most celebrated festival in China. Since 2006, the flow of railway passengers, as estimated by the Ministry of Railways, has exceeded 100 million commuters during the three weeks of what is called the "spring rush." The number increases each year due to rising rural-to-urban migration and return migrations for family reunions. Every year, around this time, the two-way traffic puts the nation's centrally controlled railway system to the test.[6] The state media names them "other-landers" (*wàidìrén*), "blind floaters" (*mángliú*), "the floating population" (*liúdòng rénkoŭ*), and "peasant-workers" (*míngōng*). They are depicted as coming in faceless "tides" (*chao*), with connotations of an uncontrollable and devastating force.

Journeying into Migrant Communities

In the summer of 2007, I spent a few months in Beijing and Shanghai doing a pilot study of rural migrant workers in preparation for my doctoral dissertation in sociology at Cornell University. I was interested in urban poverty in global cities, as well as the role of NGOs in bringing assistance to the urban poor. Using a participant observation method, I joined a few NGOs in Beijing and Shanghai and followed their teams into migrant communities. A rural migrant neighborhood in the Shijingshan district of Beijing caught my attention because of its gigantic size: the "floating population" in this urban-rural periphery of less than one square kilometers was over 40,000. It appeared to be a vast urban village. Informal businesses and migrant children schools were thriving in this area. Many male members of rural families made up the construction crew for the facilities being prepared for the summer Olympics. But by the time I revisited a year later, just before

---

6. Mitchell, "Daunting Departure." The snowstorm before the 2008 spring festival stranded over one million rural migrants in the Guangzhou city railway station alone, causing a national emergency. This event was documented by an award-winning film, *The Train to My Hometown* (2008) by Ai Xiaoming, a professor of comparative literature at Zhongshan University and an independent filmmaker.

the opening of the Olympics, this Shijingshan neighborhood was completely bulldozed. Standing on the ruins of what used to be the main market street, my NGO friend Ying said, "Twenty years from now, who will ever know that there used to be thousands of working people who labored and lived here?" She seemed to be murmuring to herself, "Their stories are never recorded, and they are gone in a minute, just like these brick houses." It was sad indeed to see the massive displacement of these families after they had contributed their labor to the proud facilities of the Beijing Olympics. Compared to the glamorous buildings of the capital city, their lives seemed so transient and invisible.

The initial motivation for this book was to record untold stories of rural migrants. I wanted to excavate the story of this massive Chinese exodus from its early years to the present. This important social change has received insufficient attention among both Chinese and western sociologists. Even among those who specialize in this topic, their writings are seldom related to the larger issues of dignity and justice. As twentieth-century British economic historian E. P. Thompson once set out "seeking to rescue the poor stockinger, the Luddite copper, the 'obsolete' hand-loom weaver, the 'utopian' artisan, and even the deluded follower of Joanna Southcott, from the enormous condescension of posterity,"[7] I desire to do the same with what happened on the Chinese scene. By recording these accounts, I want to add to the understanding of the historical torrents as well as social forces that shape the life trajectories of Chinese rural migrants. This process also made me rethink more general themes of inequality within the field of sociology. As a Christian scholar, I am not satisfied with engaging the topic only at the level of sociological phenomena. Thus, this book is also a trial attempt to engage in interdisciplinary dialogues crossing Chinese politics, human migration and Christian theology.

Many conflicts and acts of violence in today's world are related to the issue of migration, either internal or international migration. In Colombia, for example, decades of political turmoil displaced thousands of residents, who entered urban areas only

---

7. Thompson, *Making*, 12.

to find life there to be equally unsettling and violent. In Europe, many refugees from Syria enjoy only temporary shelters, and violence related to migrants breaks out in many tourist cities. In the Philippines, many women continue to migrate to other countries, often as domestic workers caring for the children of their clients, while leaving behind their own unattended children. In the United States, undocumented immigrants have suffered from systemic marginalization for decades. In China, three generations of rural migrant workers who have sacrificed greatly for the country's economic growth are becoming an underclass, excluded and alienated by both socialist and capitalist systems. These are only a few snapshots of the migration drama, but they depict the same cruel reality of rootless displacement and loss of human dignity.

The Sociology and Theology of Migration

Scholars can approach the topic of migration from different angles. Historians examine the sequence of events and contextual changes; moral philosophers spell out the obligations of individuals and the implications of their attitudes and actions; and sociologists may analyze the interplay of "push" and "pull" factors between the sending and host societies, social norms and group dynamics. In addition, theologians ponder the spiritual and pastoral implications of displaced groups. However, these specialists seldom dialogue with each other. Concerning China's internal migration problem, there has been no scholarly work bringing Christian theology to bear upon the issue.

Before writing this book, I have personally struggled for years to integrate my academic passion, sociology, with my religious devotion, the Christian faith in the Protestant tradition. In today's academic world, the discipline of sociology has its own distinct rules of the game, like most disciplines in the social sciences. Analysis of social phenomena in this discipline, almost always presented with statistical modeling, needs to be value-free and thus theology-free. Yet I am increasingly convinced that human beings are deeply moral and spiritual at the core, so questions like justice and truth are inescapable in a proper discussion of any facet of human reality. So, for a long time after the completion of my doctoral dissertation about migration, I spent years thinking about how to bridge the gaps. In writing this book, I have developed more confidence in thinking that Christian sociologists no longer need to analyze one social problem in isolation because every one of these problems goes to the core of who we are, what the world is becoming, and who God is.

My personal journey of wrestling finds partial answer in the works of a French sociologist-theologian Jacques Ellul, who produced the classic work *The Meaning of the City*. His other works also convinced me that sociology without theological depth is an incomplete enterprise, if a scholar were to be honest with oneself. Actually, theology has played a major part in the ideologies of all human cultures. On the other hand, Christian theology, when it lacks socio-historical perspective, can become depleted through over-spiritualizing exegetical practices, another form of intellectual lethargy, and weakening our thinking capacities. For example, urban poverty as a complex social reality in today's society needs careful sociological dissecting. Sociologists could contribute to this process by pinpointing the causes, which often include demographic changes, unjust economic order, poorly-defined property rights, misuse of resources, manipulation of prices, unequal pay, debt servicing, political strife, public apathy, occupational closure, workplace discrimination, etc. These are sophisticated problems that require some specialized knowledge and theories. By studying sociology, Christians could learn much about themselves (human social behavior), their churches (organizational behavior), their world (social reality) and their theology (how God's Word relates to this world). As the authors of *Our God is Undocumented* put it so well, "If our churches were to live in solidarity with the immigrant poor, we must understand the larger structural forces that first displaced them."[8]

For serious students of theology and religion, the world's changing contexts today require them to engage in an ongoing

---

8. Myers and Colwell, *Our God Is Undocumented*, 9.

INTRODUCTION

dialogue with social sciences. In my view, they will benefit from classical social theorists, such as Max Weber and Alexis de Tocqueville, because these people were wrestling with core issues of morality and spirituality for the flourishing of human beings and societies. For example, as early as a half century ago, in his *Memoir on Pauperism*, Tocqueville cautioned against legal charity because it might harm the human dignity of the poor. The moral concerns of these classic social theorists set their works in sharp contrast with contemporary sociology which deals only with technicality and fragmented social problems using what they call the "representative sampling method." If sociology as a discipline also aims to seek truth, then there needs to be more than just regression analysis.

What can sociology and theology mutually add to our understanding of migration? When different people groups are brought together by the all-encompassing capitalist economy after decades of globalization, intergroup prejudice and discrimination based on demographic or socioeconomic differences often escalates and hardens into institutionalized exclusion. Exactly how this process takes place is worthy of reflection. The sociological lens can inform us about the nature of social sin, a much-neglected topic by most Protestant thinkers today. As a Christian scholar, I also ponder what the global age of migration means for us theologically. Searching for a better life in a strange land, migrants everywhere experience the same exclusion, discrimination, exploitation, alienation, and sense of being uprooted. Migration has become an oozing wound of our time. Migration is never separate from contemporary forms of human suffering. In this sense, migration deserves not just sociological attention but also theological reflection.

The dominant narrative of the Bible is a story of migration on many levels. When the first human couple forfeited their home in Eden, rootlessness and disorientation began (Gen 3:24). Their descendants were also sojourners in foreign lands, sometimes enslaved by foreign rulers (Exod 1:10) and sometimes tragically bound by their own sin and rebellion (Judg 21:25). Yet God's loving presence also migrated with them. God explicitly stated many times that He watches over the sojourner (in Hebrew, the *gēr*). A *gēr* is the vulnerable outsider coming to live with a community. When God finally granted the Israelites a land where they could settle, He commanded that these former sojourners show compassion to new sojourners in their midst. He emphasized that they should do this because they have been there: "You were all sojourners (i.e. transient migrants) in the land of Egypt" (Deut 10:19). They were asked to remember and learn from their sojourning identity. Essentially, all of them, locals or aliens, insiders or outsiders, are spiritual refugees in this world. Later, Jesus Christ also voluntarily exiled himself to a strange world enmeshed in sin. He tasted contempt and exclusion as a member of an underclass. His apostles were all scattered to become migrating missionaries. The growth of global Christianity also witnessed voluntary migrations of Christ's witnesses to many countries. Through all of redemptive history, God shows the human race that it is not the land that makes a people "home," but God himself. The Israelites, the Tabernacle, the Temple and the body of Jesus Christ Himself all point to this final truth. Even today this remains the meta-narrative of the church, a new community that finds rootedness not in this world or any earthly citizenship, but in communion with a loving God. In the end, when we no longer sojourn, God's plan for the new humanity is a new city of righteousness (Rev 21:2).

The issue of migration is important for Christian theology. Primarily, our understanding of humankind is incomplete without trying to empathetically understand the situation of migrants in their context. Secondly, our eschatological understanding of sin, in an age of global capitalism assisted by a type of technological tyranny (in Ellul's terms), is incomplete without an adequate examination of social and institutional sins. Thirdly, the unity of the church is incomplete when she fails to effectively pastor members who experience the pains of migration. A dialogue between sociology and Christian theology can be instrumental in fulfilling these tasks. It would enable us to gain a systematic picture of structural changes and the accompanying social and psychological changes. Moreover, sociology also equips us with a situational empathy. It is this empathy which motivates a Christian scholar to study the context of his or her neighbors. After this analytical step, there also needs to be moral theology to guide us. Regarding the urban poor, generally speaking, poverty as a fact of life deserves to be examined from a theological lens. Extreme poverty inhibits freedom, which is at the core of what it means to be a human being. What God intends for us is flourishing, or *shalom*. More importantly, poverty deprives humans of dignity. So, my main purpose in this book is to formulate a socio-theological hermeneutic of migrant experiences and urban poverty in contemporary China.

Ethical Implications

How can Christian ethics respond to the misery imposed by the human experience of migration and poverty? How can "loving your neighbor" be practically applied? First of all, according to Scripture, in the end times when systemic injustice increases, Christians have an obligation of conscience: their love for justice should not grow cold (Matt 24:12). The circumstances of the poor should still prick their consciences. They should not consider it normal or commonplace. In fact, they should retain an indignation at the injustice done to the poor. They need to begin by fighting the war against indifference and ignorance. When Jesus himself said that "the poor you will always have with you" (Mark 14:7), this is better understood as a statement about the lasting relevance of poverty to the church. God seems to have a bias to the poor, as many Catholic teachings term it "the preference for the poor," and we should too. But first, one needs to inform his or her consciousness by understanding the origins of these problems. At this point, sociological knowledge of the problem becomes necessary. Racism, sexism, marginalization and classism do matter to Christians, because these communal attitudes and structures oppress others and deprive them of human dignity. In a sense, emotional activism or situational empathy is needed in Christians' approach to migrants caught in structural poverty.

In a country like China where churches, NGOs and charity organizations are suppressed, it is more difficult to carry out organized efforts to help.[9] Yet there are still creative and small-scale ministries to help the marginalized. A range of questions have to be wrestled with before formulating any action plans. This primarily means to "know the stranger" first by asking a series of questions: What kind of unjust institutions and social processes have shaped the experiences of migrants and their poverty? How have individuals responded to or internalized these social sins to make them perpetual? What resources are there in our theological tradition that would shed light on relevant issues such as displacement, urban prejudice and alienation? In this book, I attempt to answer these questions instead of suggesting practical strategies for action.

The second ethical implication for Christians in an age of migration is to practice genuine hospitality. The command to "love the stranger" occurs thirty-six times in the Old Testament alone. Hospitality defines the social attitude of Christians toward others and community-building. True hospitality takes the situational vulnerability of the stranger into consideration.

Public discourse so often centers on the utility of migrant population—whether they are a benefit or a burden to a local economy—that most people are used to such dehumanizing rhetoric as if migrants are construction materials. In doing so, they ignore the core of the question—what makes a human being human, and what is human dignity? Genuine hospitality should have the respect for others' dignity at its core. Classical theorist Alexis de Tocqueville has modeled for Christians and sociologists in this respect how to integrate sociological analysis with ethical concerns.

A third ethical implication of theologizing migration requires Christians to trust in the justice and sovereignty of God. Such a trust will give wisdom to our understanding of the whole migration picture. God not only gave the promised land to ancient Israelites, He did, in fact, give lands to all tribes and people. With the eyes of faith, Christians believe that everything happens according to

---

9. Ma and Li, *Surviving the State*, 106–18.

INTRODUCTION

God's sovereign plan. This lifts us up from despair, and it also grants us moral responsibility to actively respond to social problems.

Organization of the Book

This book offers a sociological analysis as well as a theological discussion of China's internal migration. I historically document the social and political processes that parallel the experiences of rural-to-urban migrants. Institutional change, social attitudes, and ethical reflections are woven together in each phase of migration experiences. Some chapters are more sociological than theological, and some are the other way around.

Chapter 2 offers a historical account of China's internal migration as an instituted process during and after communist central planning. I use both archival data and interviews with rural migrants to construct the political, economic and social dimensions of the creation of an underclass. Chapter 3 discusses the urban context into which rural migrants relocate. Market forces are utilized by a watchful communist state to create a double demoralization effect on urban society. As a system engulfing the worth of human beings, China's economy deems workers as mere "human capital." I reflect on how migrants' human personhood and self-esteem are being challenged with these disorienting materialistic and consumeristic values. Chapter 4 documents the tragic loss of community in rural migrants' neighborhoods. The disintegration of family togetherness and loss of neighborliness adds another level of alienation to the migrant experience. I conclude by discussing the significance and fragility of human community. Chapter 5 highlights the experiences of NGO workers and other good Samaritans who try to ameliorate the effects of social injustice by a variety of creative programs in which they also encounter tremendous challenges. I also reflect on the role of Chinese Christians in reaching out to rural migrants and the possibility of community rebuilding among them. In the concluding chapter, I summarize on the larger themes of globalization and social justice.

2

The Regime and the Underclass

> The more equal conditions are, the less explanation there is for the differences that actually exist between people; and thus all the more unequal do individuals and groups become. This perplexing consequence came fully to light as soon as equality was no longer seen in terms of an omnipotent being like God or an unavoidable common destiny like death.
>
> —Hannah Arendt

DURING THE LUNAR NEW Year, the average Chinese citizen realizes the presence of the "floating population," as it is officially labeled, for several reasons besides the experience of overcrowding on long-distance train rides. It is a time when wage arrears and exploitations of rural migrants receive wider attention through the state media, sometimes with reports of top communist leaders helping them to claim back their overdue earnings.[1] It is often a time when some urban residents of large cities warn each other about higher crime rates, pointing to the potential criminality of rural migrants in certain migrant-concentrated neighborhoods.

China's massive rural-to-urban migration has brought sweeping social change to its society. In 1984, after agricultural de-collectivization and the collapse of people's communes in rural areas, the central government deregulated control over the

---

1. In the spring of 2003, a rural migrant woman named Xiong Deming made a direct claim to Premier Wen Jiabao while he was on an inspection trip to her hometown about a 2300 yuan wage arrears her husband suffered. See "Migrant Workers: Urban Underclass."

residential mobility of peasants, allowing them entry to non-farming jobs in townships and cities. Thus, migrating peasants no longer faced severe penalties for leaving the countryside. With deepening economic reforms, market incentives also encouraged enterprises to recruit cheap rural labor, first into township undertakings in the 1980s and then into urban industrial enterprises during the 1990s. As a result of gradual deregulation, the number of rural workers migrating from their villages tripled from twenty million to sixty million in less than a decade until the early 1990s.[2] In the following decade, China's landscape witnessed the biggest peacetime wave of internal migration the world has ever seen. By 2007, half of the Chinese population become city-dwellers, compared to just 20 percent in 1985.

During this time, however, the longstanding rural-urban income gap in China not only persisted, but worsened, when compared to most other developing countries.[3] Statistically, the poverty rate among rural migrants is fifty percent higher than among urban residents.[4] Remnants of China's socialist institutions, after the gradualist market reform, continue to stratify rural migrants and their next generation through sociopolitical processes. Making up two-thirds of the labor force nowadays in China, rural migrants experience social forces due to China's emerging market capitalism, as well as repercussions from its socialist legacy.

Rural migrants and urban residents have been classified into two different forms of citizenship that were deeply rooted in the ideological and organizational structures of Chinese socialism. Therefore, economic liberalization itself did little to promote upward mobility for rural migrants. Changes in formal rules interact with the persistence of informal forces—customs, networks, norms, and cultural beliefs—to produce persistent structures of exclusion. Rural migrants respond to these constraints by developing distinctive coping strategies at work, in the community, and

---

2. Chan, *Cities with Invisible Walls*; Liang, "Age of Migration," 499–524.

3. Knight et al., "Rural-Urban Divide"; Eastwood and Lipton, "Rural and Urban Income Inequality."

4. Yusuf and Saich, *China Urbanizes*, 94.

in family life. However, despite their efforts, rural migrants are treated as a caste of permanent transients in the city.

Shadow of the Old Regime

Rural migrants come to cities carrying historical baggage from China's past. Their lives and identities are trapped in a time capsule of the old regime, extending as far back as the feudal age. How then was the system (now known as *hukou*) that locks peasants into a perpetual low status established in the first place? What are the sources of inertia which make it so durable over time? *Hukou*, China's citizenship identification system and her backbone institution, affected fundamental aspects of life for millions of Chinese, especially during the central planning era. How the "iron curtain" of *hukou* control was institutionalized, and how the *hukou* order retained a lasting grip on social stratification in the post-socialist era require a close examination of that history.

Systems of household-based registration originated in the Xia Dynasty (2070–1600 BC) along with a population census and, according to *Shiji*, also known as Records of the Great Historian. When Qin unified China (221 BC), a *baojia* system (sometimes spelled as *pao-chia*) was adopted nationally,[5] and its application to taxation and conscription was expanded and reinforced. Individuals were required to report residence, age, gender, and profession to the ruler, who verified such information three times a year. A functional system of population registration identified a person as a resident of a region and included his or her basic personal information into document files. A household was usually registered into one document: the *huji*, later known as *"hu-kou"* (literally combining the terms for "household" and "mouth"). Historically, given the vast farming population among the Chinese, the system was born of a marriage between totalitarian politics and agrarian order. The dynastic cycles after the

---

5. It was a community-based system of law enforcement and civil control created during the Song Dynasty.

Qin brought changes to the *huji* system, but its functions in tax collection and law enforcement persisted.

Despite the presence of social control, internal migration of peasants persisted during those eras. Even with legal prohibitions, local enforcement by the gentry class was weak. Thus, *hukou* records merely became inaccurate as in the Sui and Tang dynasties discovered, when bureaucratic appointments were made through the imperial exam system, which was linked up with household registration. It was not until the Sui and especially the Tang Dynasty (AD 581–907) when the *huji* system was incorporated into the imperial political apparatus. Bureaucratic offices were set up, and master *huji* files were created and maintained. Individuals were classified into four main categories: military, peasants, merchants, and handicraft workers. They were each subjected to different tax burdens. This highly bureaucratized feature was passed on to subsequent regimes, including the rulers of the Republic China and the People's Republic of China. In fact, maintenance of the *huji* records became one of the evaluation criteria for government officials. Reforms in the subsequent Ming and Qing dynasties severed the traditional links between taxation and the old *huji* system. A *baojia* system replaced *huji*, but it incorporated even stricter forms of social surveillance.

As a result, traditional Chinese society has displayed a pronounced hierarchical structure with individuals falling into various ranks. The Chinese have become habituated to such differentiated citizenships. As Fairbank and Goldman note, the Chinese people have long developed a vision of the ruler as the "dispenser of justice" who has "inherited control" over the peasantry:

> In China's inheritance was the tradition that the state authorities had unquestioned control over the populace in the villages (e.g. the *pao-chia* system, *li-chia* system). Using these structures, emperors from early times had pursued public works using labor conscripted from the countryside. The ruling class in short could tell the peasants what to do with himself and his belongings at the same time they taxed him . . . Part of China's inheritance

was that their state of morale, their loyalty to the center, was a key determinant of the results achieved.[6]

China's rural-urban gap has had a long history as well. Historian Frederick W. Mote notices "a cultural continuum of country and city" discernible in traditional China.[7] Skinner observes a complex web that includes "markers of economic, political, and cultural divergence" between villages and cities.[8] The rural-urban gap persisted since the majority of the Chinese lived on farmland, but rural migrants were also a common presence in cities. Cohen points out that urban intellectuals "invented" the cultural category of Chinese peasantry in the early twentieth century.[9] Mann claims that "urban bias" was emerging in the 1920s and 1930s, as urbanites developed different views of their "rural roots."[10]

The great demarcation between rural and urban society, nevertheless, took place only after communist rule. Although Chinese peasantry had long been considered as an inherited social status, peasants were then free to enter into mercantile trading or the political elite group through the *keju* exam system. It is important to note that it was during the communist Great Leap Forward (1958–1961) that China made a qualitative transformation into a rural-urban hierarchy along *hukou* lines. Communist collectivization enforced inherited status, place-based identities, entitlement to necessities, and collectivist norms. Never had *hukou* control penetrated to such a totalitarian degree in China.

During the Chinese civil war in the 1930s, food scarcity was widespread. When rice provisions fell short, the Republic of China government enacted food rationing. The rationing system heightened village-city relations. For the first time in China's

---

6. Fairbank and Goldman, *China: A New History*, 368.
7. Mote, "City in Traditional Chinese Civilization," 42–49.
8. Skinner, *City in Late Imperial China*, 267–69.
9. Cohen, "Cultural and Political Inventions," 151.
10. Urban elites projected three paths for rural development: a "nativist" celebration of rural roots, a "reconstructionist" approach to revive the countryside, and a "positive" perspective urging urbanization. See Mann, "Urbanization and Historical Change," 94.

history, political actors allocated food rationing based on *hukou* registration. In Shanghai, for example, rationed rice gained the name of "*hukou* rice" (*hukou mi*), as only Shanghai *hukou*-holders were entitled to it. By such stringent rules of food provision, the government "successfully" discouraged rural migrants from seeking urban shelter. This "temporary" wartime policy was a crucial development because it reshaped the entitlement hierarchy among people. Such "institutional genesis" left unintended consequences. Although the design can be "tentative" at the time of urgency, it often produces lasting ramifications—state power penetrated the society with new techniques of social control.[11]

Rationing requires uniformity and elaborate checks against evasion. These policies transform political structures, social relationships and attitudes. If the design of a rationing system fails to neutralize the existing privileges by giving more to advantaged groups, or if it is based on criteria other than nutritional need, it tends to twist the redistributive system toward injustice. Instead of using rationing to alleviate the effects of class, it becomes twisted into a strategy of exclusion. In the case of China, new categories of social status were invented, by which a sense of "unworthiness" was attached to those excluded. Furthermore, scarcity also tends to create a panic to guard one's membership among the privileged. As Weber points out, resource scarcity and competition are the preconditions for closure-formation based on "externally identifiable characteristics."[12]

In other social contexts, famines and plagues sometimes gave rise to similar processes of institutional genesis. At the end of the seventeenth century, France adopted methods of registration in some plagued towns to discourage internal migration.[13] The "momentary" nature of this form of social control functioned only for that time period. Temporary sacrifice of fair distribution is dangerous, but it would lead to more damaging effects if such a rationing system were enacted for a prolonged period. Unfortunately,

11. Anderson, "Food Rationing and Morale," 23–33
12. Weber, *Economy and Society*, 342.
13. Foucault, *Discipline and Punish*, 144.

the food shortage crisis and urban unemployment in China lasted longer than the civil war, and even throughout communist rule. The Chinese civil war and the subsequent regime change to communism in the 1940s created a historic opportunity for the new regime to launch large-scale social engineering.

After 1949, high unemployment and inflation plagued the country's war-battered economy. The number of unemployed people and refugees amounted to 1.66 million in nine large cities. Shanghai alone had 150,000 urban residents without jobs.[14] A news editorial in 1949 asserted that "Shanghai can only maintain a population of three million."[15] In the early 1950s, Shanghai administrators urged jobless family members of hundreds of thousands of residents to return to the countryside. Massive numbers of wartime refugees and jobless migrants eventually moved from large cities to resettle in the countryside.

Migration-control developed into a fully established system forbidding freedom of movement only after 1958. It was the main component of the Chinese Communism project, which later brought disastrous outcomes. Scott summarizes four areas in which some full-fledged statecrafts fail:

1. the administrative ordering of nature and society,
2. a high-modernist ideology,
3. an authoritarian state that is willing and able to use the full weight of its coercive power to bring these high-modernist designs into being, and
4. a prostrate civil society that lacks the capacity to resist these plans.[16]

He points out that wartime shortages and revolutions make "the most fertile soil" for the state to use its coercive power to realize its designs:

---

14. Quoted in Zeng and Lin, *New China Economic History*, 19.
15. Cited in Gaulton, "Political Mobilization," 46.
16. Scott, *Seeing Like a State*, 4.

In such situations, emergency conditions foster the seizure of emergency powers and frequently delegitimatize the previous regime. They also "give rise to elites who repudiate the past and who have revolutionary designs for their people."[17]

The evolution of *hukou* was an inevitable outcome of a Soviet type of central planning system moving toward heavy industrialization, which required meticulous control of all resources, especially labor flows. The Soviet Union initiated the archetypical internal passport system, "*the propiska*" (1932–1974), to separate the rural population from the urban. The *propiska* quota was used to control the influx of non-native residents into a few major cities. That system was not abolished until the collapse of the Soviet Union. Similar systems existed in other communist societies, such as Vietnam (*ho khau*) and present-day North Korea (*hoju*). These societies share common experiences in dealing with resource scarcity, and they were all influenced by the Soviet economic model.

The Making of the Underclass

At the founding of the People's Republic of China in 1949, China was predominantly an agrarian society. Driven by an ideological zeal to eliminate class differences, communist leaders pushed for violent methods of land reform. The early 1950s witnessed the most sweeping land reforms in world history. Reclassification of people was aimed at elevating the oppressed above the privileged class. Wealth gaps were artificially equalized, and the existing landlord class was wiped out by force. To a large extent, these political movements helped the communist party gain nationwide allegiance from the nation's large base of peasants.

Reclassification reinforced the social boundaries of wealth and class. More tragically, it legitimatized the social classification of inherited status. The children of poor peasantry were considered politically upright, while the descendants of wealthier

---

17. Scott, *Seeing Like a State*, 5.

families had a lasting stigma impressed upon them. This gave rise to a stratification mentality based on birthright among all Chinese. This inherited feature of class stratification has had a lasting impact on how the Chinese viewed each other in terms of relative social standings during the socialist era. It also contributed to how people received the inherited characteristic *hukou* status as an "appropriate" social distinction.

Ascribed status is the social standing an individual is assigned at birth or assumed by tradition or law. Lower strata of such a status hierarchy are often inseparable from the negative stereotypes associated with them. All societies display such practices of assigning certain status based on sex, gender, race, family origins, and ethnic differences. The Chinese *hukou* system imposed a unique type of status upon individuals by parents' place of residence, a structural rarity across cultures. Over time, *hukou* has become a deeply ingrained socio-cultural identity people use in constructing stereotypes. Before the late 1980s, a person's *hukou* membership could be "transferred" only through marriage, military service or entering a college. In some situations, revoking a previously held urban *hukou* status was used as an additional punishment for imprisoned criminals.

The 1950s witnessed a series of cyclical policy changes that tightened and loosened controls on migration. Inconsistency and ambivalence caused great institutional uncertainty. As early as 1953, the state implemented a "Unified Purchase and Sale" (*tong gou tong xiao*) policy to eliminate market mechanisms in determining prices. Only the state had the power to purchase and sell grains, and private market activities were prohibited. The state used "price scissors" (*jiandao cha*) to artificially lower the prices of agricultural products and to keep industrial goods at higher prices. By doing so, the state could transfer resources efficiently. Another goal of this policy was to restrict food consumption through central plans. Rural and urban collectives were supposed to provide food on a rationed basis. When both food allocation and pricing mechanisms were legitimized to achieve planned goals, a vast chasm was created between agricultural production and industrial production. Politically, it was a clear-cut resolution to separate the two classes. A central directive in November of 1955 entitled "Criteria for the Demarcation between Urban and Rural Areas" officially imposed a geographical hierarchy.

Of all public policies, economist Michael Lipton argues that the "price-twists" hurt the interests of the rural class most.[18] In the process, this class lost its competitiveness in international agricultural markets. Similar measures to distort pricing mechanisms were used in many other developing countries during the 1950s. When nations adopt this ideology of urban-industrial developmentalism, unequal exchanges between rural and urban residents lead to a social norm of "urban bias" within these societies. Usually, this tendency of urban bias is most evident in the provision of education and other public welfare spending decisions. In China, administrative authorities set up urban *danwei* (work unit) systems and rural communes as production units. Prices for raw materials and labor were pre-set. From the beginning, these two groups were given different entitlements. Urban residents were identified as direct contributors to industrialization, so their political loyalty was to be secured with stable rewards. In contrast, the needs of rural residents were deemed less urgent.

In their efforts to make the central plan work, communist leaders constantly feared political sabotage. This fear drove them toward a system of identification that proved one's political loyalty whenever mobility was concerned. Even cadre-party-members who traveled to places other than their *danwei* were expected to carry a stack of reference letters with them, including proof of party membership, administrative references, food and oil references, etc. A *People's Daily* article illustrates the importance of *hukou* identification to socialist stability: "When class conflicts are becoming increasingly sharp these days, we must improve *hukou* management, in order to fill up the cracks that may create opportunities for hidden enemies to use legal identities for sabotage."[19] But rational planning in grain allocation did not stop

---

18. Lipton, *Why Poor People Stay Poor*.
19. "Do Not Fill in Wrong Information," para. 6.

peasants from migrating to cities through personal connections. To cope with the limited food distribution problem, a "grey" labor market emerged in eastern Beijing in 1955. Peasant-led anti-collectivization movements peaked in 1956, resulting in widespread violence in rural areas.

Official documents show that starting in 1953, the central government issued decrees to "persuade" peasants not to "blindly" flow into cities. They used several techniques to prepare for the total abolition of population movement through *hukou* legislation: "thought work" (*sixiang gongzuo*), role models, and mobilization for returning to rural areas. Persuasive methods were developed by the communists in Yan'an city. There they had set up a Stalinist command economy where peasants were requisitioned according to their economic plans. The communist propaganda machine played a significant role. Firstly, they successfully elevated the Soviet-type state socialism into a blueprint for desireable "modernization." Secondly, reports, pictures, and stories were mass produced to transmit social and political values that fundamentally changed people's thinking and behaviors.

Ironically, the idea of "worker-peasant alliance" propagated by the communists served to lock peasants into second-class membership. After founding the regime, Mao and many other communist leaders reckoned that the Party should not allow peasants to lead another revolution. Therefore, peasants needed to be educated and regulated.

In support of communist developmental goals, peasants living with urban relatives (who were termed the "fostered population") were mobilized to return to the countryside. In Taiyuan city, for example, 56.6 percent of the total resident population belonged to the "fostered population" (*bei fuyang renkou*) in August of 1957. The city government determined to "mobilize" ten thousand "nonproductive individuals" (*fei shengchan renyuan*) to return to rural areas. These people included temporarily hired workers, rural migrants from famine areas, and homemakers and dependents of urban workers. However, even some individuals working in service sectors were considered redundant.

The above terminology depicted rural migrants as dependent, nonproductive, directly making a causal connection between their presence in the city and the deterioration of city infrastructure and worsened food shortages.[20] Non-coercive and "voluntary" programs were designed to achieve such reallocation, including persuasion and positive incentives for return. Little resistance occurred because few people foresaw any barriers for them to re-enter the cities in the future. All levels of party organs, including the Ministry of Civil Affairs, the Ministry of Labor, the Ministry of Food, the Communist Youth League, and the Women's Union formed work teams that specialized in "persuading" peasants to return. The goal was to "compress urban population."

This movement to effect mass mobilization not only implied the state's determination to implement the plan for strict labor allocation, but also that urban employment was in a crisis too deep to tolerate any labor input from rural areas. Policy makers assumed that labor reallocation to the countryside could work, because rural lands could provide at least basic living necessities at lower cost. Urban employment was considered a top priority because urban industries were the engines for China's economic growth. As Friedrich Hayek classically stated, because socialist planners do not have feasible clear-cut plans to realize their grand picture of a utopia, they usually "manipulate the economy so that the distribution of incomes will be made to conform to their conception of social justice."[21] Unfortunately, few policy-makers were equipped with enough social science knowledge to foresee any disastrous social outcomes.

On January 10, 1958, the state passed the PRC *Hukou* Registration Regulations; thus, a formal law separating rural and urban boundaries (geographical and occupational) was officially established. Until that day, it remains the only legal document that had been passed by China's highest legislative body, the People's Congress. It required that rural peasants obtain legal papers before migrating, and the legalization process was tightly controlled.

20. "Mobilize Nonproductive Individuals to Return."
21. Hayek, *Constitution of Liberty*, 372.

Articles 15 and 16 stipulated that rural residents needed to go through legal procedures if they planned to stay for more than three days in cities. Enforcement offices encompassing public security, food bureaus, and public transportation were all assigned different roles to impose strict *hukou* control. Meanwhile, food rationing was strictly enforced in cities, so anyone lacking legal registration could not obtain subsistence goods. The over-arching goal was to deter rural-to-urban migration.

Following the 1958 legislation, even transfer of *hukou* status from the "agricultural" category to "nonagricultural" was strictly prohibited. The only legitimate mobility channels were limited to attending universities, joining the military, or marrying someone from another region. Visitors and temporary migrants were required to register with the local *hukou* police for permission to stay. In 1964, the Ministry of Public Security issued a "decree" (*tiaoli*) forbidding peasants from migrating into townships. In the 1975 constitutional amendment acts, the People's Congress, China's then-legislative body, historically eliminated the "freedom of residential mobility and migration" from the Chinese Constitution. During subsequent constitutional amendments (1980, 1982 and 2004), this freedom has never been restored. Over time, the Household Registration System has increasingly evolved into "an internal *de facto* passport mechanism," blocking peasants from upward mobility and creating a pattern of "internal colonization" within a nation.

The rigidity of forced rural collectivization culminated in the greatest famine in human history, with a death toll of over thirty million during the years between 1958 and 1961, historically known as the Great Famine. Statistics show that most deaths were reported in rural areas, where peasants were not permitted to move outside their failing communes, not even to beg for food. Fairbank argues that "this organization of the countryside was far more complete than anything previously attempted in Chinese history."[22]

---

22. Fairbank, *Great Chinese Revolution*, 284.

The subsequent political movements in 1960s and 1970s reinforced the rural-urban divide. In 1961, with an urban economic crisis and unemployment becoming more intense, the state directed an anti-urbanization movement, known as the "send-down of urban educated youth." It was also aimed at easing urban unemployment and increasing agricultural productivity. But communist propaganda idealized this movement as a collective effort to smooth out "three major differences," namely the differences between agricultural and industrial production, between rural and urban, and between manual and non-manual work. This movement had a lasting social impact on the Chinese society by sharpening the status differences between peasants and urban workers. It continued during the most turbulent years of the Chinese Cultural Revolution, when over twenty million urban secondary school graduates were "exiled" to poor rural areas. Real life experiences show clashes between these "sent-down" urbanites and villagers, intensifying the enmity between these two groups. Almost every urban family suffered the trauma of long-term separation. Because a small number of urban elites secured the quota for returning youth, those with weak political connections had to endure years of exile in remote rural areas. An urban *hukou* was viewed as a passport out of exile and misery. Many sent-down youth committed suicide after they failed to qualify as part of the urban *hukou* quota. Although state propaganda promoted this movement as "re-education by peasants," in reality, it created a larger chasm between the rural peasantry and urban citizens.

After the downfall of the Gang of Four in 1976, millions of sent-down youth requested a return to their urban homes. However, over the course of intensive political movements, the state, as a social control machine, had gained considerable power in selectively recruiting politically loyal members. It enforced difficult "screening" procedures to check the returning flows. Some made it back to colleges or the military through personal connections. Others returned to join the urban labor force. In addition, special policies were made to allow those needing medical treatment to return. Almost twenty years after the send-down movement, there was another wave of "returning to the city," although at a much smaller scale. The increased costs of return, to a large extent, reinforced the superiority of an urban residential status. Sixty-five-year-old Lin, originally a Beijing resident, was sent down to rural Heilongjiang in 1963 when he was fifteen years old, and it was not until 1998 that he finally returned to the city after retirement. He recalled the stringent rules "sent-down youth" had to pass before getting permission to return to the city of their original residence. Merit-based college entrance examination resumed only by the end of 1977. It offered a slightly more objective criterion for many sent-down youths to return to urban areas. Getting higher education gained popularity among rural young people too, because it was one way to obtain urban residence after graduation.

Since the late 1970s, the reemergence of trading markets increased momentum for peasants to obtain non-farming jobs. In 1979, some peasants from Hebei swarmed Beijing selling various agricultural products on the streets. The scale of street vending grew to such proportions that the Industrial and Commerce Bureau and Public Security Bureau of Beijing city decided to set up ten marketplaces in Beijing's suburbs for them. With more freedom for market activities between the onset of economic reform (1978) and the legal relaxation of migration control (1984), the out-migration of peasants continued at a small scale. Transfers of *hukou* status were made possible only through application and approval by local governments. During this time, some rural cadres engaged in "*hukou* trafficking"—selling urban *hukou* designations as commodities so that these *hukou*-holders could freely relocate.

Rural *hukou*-holders also gradually entered the urban labor market, creating some region-specific services. My fieldwork interviews show that some pioneering rural migrants included vegetable-vendors from Shandong, domestic maids from Anhui, cooks from Sichuan, etc. The five years between 1978 and 1983 saw streams of "illegitimate" rural out-migration. The collective memories of being labelled, channeled and needing to hide from authorities still haunt the older demographic of rural migrants nowadays. Unlike the experiences of the educated youth, who tasted the banishment of downward *hukou* mobility, migrants in these years faced a rigid form of legal punishment to keep them "disciplined." Such types of discipline developed a hidden order of social surveillance. When their intention to escape the misery of socialist planning conflicted with the motherland's "expectation" for them, these citizens internalized a sense of disloyalty and guilt into their self-concepts.

To socialist legislators, uncontrolled population mobility represented disorder and a potential threat to regime stability. This view was so widely held in the 1980s that it almost became a legal paranoia that perceived any individual action as irrational and subversive. The word "*mangliu*" (blindly floating waves) refers to people who wonder around without fix jobs. During my fieldwork in 2009, local administrators still used this derogatory term to refer to rural migrants.

Mass Migration

Six years after economic reform in 1984, with forces in the economy pushing and pulling for disintegration, the rural-urban wall of residential immobility began to crack. The internal opening-up process for China began. The state formally relaxed *Hukou*, by legally permitting peasants to freely move into townships with self-provided food. It marked the end of serf-like ties to the land that Chinese peasants experienced during the Mao period. Since migrant trends follow a cumulative pattern, a small dent in the dam could result in a flood, especially when the water level had been approaching a crest a long time ago. Jobs, housing and public facilities became increasingly accessible to whoever could afford them.

Also in 1984, rural communes were dismantled and restructured into rural industrial units. Peasants were incorporated into non-farming jobs. The decade from 1984 to 1994 was the golden age for township and village enterprises (TVEs). When privatization of the economy was still frowned upon as "politically incorrect," these TVEs served dual interests, both as private economic initiatives and as political entrepreneurship in the growing commodity market. However, their failure was also immediate. With increased market competition and the growth of private firms, the TVE sector shrank into recession. Since then, even more rural migrants ventured into cities. At first, most of them were permitted to migrate and then return only on a short-term basis. Because the old food ration system was still present in many cities, these migrants had to purchase daily necessities at higher price from native residents when they ran out of their own provisions. It was not until 1993 when the food ration system was abolished.

Overall, the years between 1978 to 1994 marked a time during which state officials wavered and delayed making public policies concerning rural-urban migration. Public attitudes toward the presence of rural migrants in cities were still largely hostile. When urban residents or administrators met rural migrants in the city, they tended to accuse them of abandoning their "socialist duty" of farming in the countryside. The general public was resistant to breaking down the rigid social categorization inherited from the planning era.

After the state made a progressive move to allow rural peasants to legally transfer their residence status to the township's "non-agricultural" category, local governments began to sell *hukous*, in essence using them to function as "green cards."[23] Despite the state's continued campaign against these underground activities, some *hukou* black markets are still active even today. According to the China Newsweek, a Beijing *hukou* was priced to 150,000 yuan for someone with a Master's degree and double major certificates. Responding to the question of who were more likely to get these deals, the seller responded: "It's easier for people with science degrees and other urgently-needed majors to get Beijing *hukou*, but not for those in the arts."[24]

---

23. Green cards or work visas are only analogies for the identification system of foreigners in some countries. But even if *hukou* can be compared to them, it still exerts constraint to all other areas of life, including housing, education, medical care, and other social services.

24. The news article "Why Have Prices Jumped for Beijing *Hukous*?" reported a finding from a survey on the *hukou* market conducted by the *China Youth Newspaper* in 2008. It showed that seventy percent of buyers wanted

Abuse and Advocacy

Since the plight of rural migrants has been brought to wider public attention, some conscientious intellectuals and civil rights activists have advocated for legislative changes. Debates around whether or not to abolish the caste-like *Hukou* system began in the early 1990s. Some local governments did respond with "timelines" for abolition, but no implementation followed. Hopes were stirred, but then new policies always fell short of the expectations of the majority, because cities tend to welcome the "haves" (the rich and educated) rather than the "have-nots." Across China, every city-level government has used *hukou* to "handpick" a small number of migrant applicants into its system. Meanwhile, the scale of rural-urban migration has continued to soar each year. Rural migrants' mobility, rootlessness, "ruralness" of appearance and their seeming craze for monetary gains have been suspect as a potential for criminality.[25] It was amid such a hostile environment that rent-seeking urban administrators combined arbitrary fees and violence to afflict low-status rural migrants.

A tragic but milestone event happened on April 25 of 2003 when Sun Zhigang, a twenty-seven-year-old graduate student was mistaken for a rural migrant worker and died of abuse at Guangzhou city's deportation center. Sun was detained for carrying no "temporary residence permit" and was then beaten to death. This news story caused public outrage on the Internet. The Custody and Deportation System, established since 1982, has gradually changed into a rent-seeking and rapacious system for urban administrators to target rural migrants. The use of violence was central in the institutionalization of *hukou* by the powerful yet secretive public security agents.

The following May, three independent legal professionals submitted a petition against the Detention and Deportation System. On June 20, 2003, the State Council announced the abolition

---

Beijing *hukou* for its "access to value added resources," such as health care, housing and education.

25. Zhang, *Strangers in the City*.

of this system. The high-profile incident and the abolitionist efforts marked the watershed of the government's attitude toward rural migrants. Since 2003, China's media switched to a sympathizing tone toward their plight, from wage arrears and slave labor, to hate crimes committed by rural migrants, due to marginalization. However, it was only in recent years when issues of social justice and equal rights for rural migrants entered into public discussion. The government made a few commendable steps after reckoning with the dire reality of injustice toward rural migrants. In early 2005, the Ministry of Labor and Social Security abolished the existing "Interim Stipulations on Interprovincial Rural Migration" (enacted since 1998), the institutional foundation for collecting fees from rural migrants. The state has publicly addressed the inadequacies in social services as well as the unfairness of their distribution among urban and rural citizens. Announcements to provide rural health care, free compulsory education, and a rural minimum living stipend, however, await implementation. In 2005, the Ministry of Public Security announced a legal review of the *hukou* system, but it later decided that changes ought to be made by local governments. Yet, it is precisely among local governments that resistance against further reform is strongest, because granting equal rights to rural migrants would mean higher public expenditures and additional funding to provide education, health care and other social services. Under the current system, urbanization becomes simply another opportunity for local governments to exploit the utility of *hukou*.

Why did unjust institutions persist that deprive rural migrants of their basic rights? Waves of political movements have cemented the urban elite into an interest alliance which includes bureaucrats, technocrats, politicians and even intellectuals. Collectively, they control both the ideological and technological tools for resource allocation that, in turn, bring them economic benefits. As Max Weber claims, the durability of power in systems of domination is primarily determined by those who were involved in the enforcement of power.[26] This system of domination brands

26. Weber, *Economy and Society*, 214.

spontaneous activities as belonging to "defiant," "rule-breaking" elements, which require coercion and even criminalization. Furthermore, such rigid social categorization tends to create impersonal and legitimate labels for bureaucrats to manipulate. Their activities gave rise to "increasing returns mechanisms" that perpetuate social distinctions.

Marketization inevitably challenges such rigid social distinctions, because it requires more fluidity. Economic restructuring in China has transformed the authority relations between classes. Opportunities opened up to people and their economic prospects were no longer confined by public institutions. Inflows of displaced socialist peasants into the cities challenged the old "public goods regime" of the socialist social contract.[27] In theory, instituting *hukou* as a price mechanism is not compatible with a market system. However, China's landscape of rural-urban inequality is becoming more worrisome. Urbanization with partial market reform created contradictory assimilating and segregating mechanisms for rural migrants' integration into urban society. The social distinction based on *hukou* continued to allocate certain resources inequitably (e.g. education, health, housing, etc), because rent-creation through the assignment of exclusive rights and privileges lies at the heart of this type of social structure.

Theological Reflections: Institutionalized Exclusion as Social Sin

How should we read this history? We can give a similar answer to the one offered by Russian writer Aleksandr Solzhenitsyn that it is about the failure of a whole social system that lauded human capacity and abandoned God. But what else can Christian theology offer in thinking about the communist regime and its logic for economic planning? It is indeed ironic that communism not only failed to produce a classless society, it instead created and perpetuated a structured inequality. But what is the spiritual lesson behind

---

27. Solinger, "China's Urban Transients."

this irony? Are individuals merely victims of systemic suppression? To what extent are individuals accountable?

Christian theology needs to reformulate the problem of evil in the context of economic planning and bureaucratization of the modern nation-state. As Max Weber phrases it, a state is a human community that (successfully) claims the monopoly of the legitimate use of physical force within a given territory.[28] Thus, the state claims the right to support itself through *force*. In other words, the state claims that it does not have to follow the same rules as other individuals and institutions in a civilized society. Institutionalized exclusion through depriving a certain classified group of access to economic resources produces a lasting impact on society. Its normalization of injustice through policy-making creates irreversible damage to the social order, because as Reinhold Niebuhr claims in his classic *Moral Man and Immoral Society*, social structures and norms, once set in place, are utterly rigid and thus harmful in perpetuating injustice.

> Individual men may be moral in the sense that they are able to consider interests other than their own in determining problems of conduct, and are capable, on occasion, of preferring the advantages of others to their own. They are endowed by nature with a measure of sympathy and consideration for their kind, the breadth of which may be extended by an astute social pedagogy. Their rational faculty prompts them to a sense of justice which educational discipline may refine and purge of egoistic elements until they are able to view a social situation, in which their own interests are involved, with a fair measure of objectivity. But all these achievements are more difficult, if not impossible, for human societies and social groups. In every human group there is less reason to guide and to check impulse, less capacity for self-transcendence, less ability to comprehend the needs of others and therefore more unrestrained egoism than

---

28. Weber, "Politics as Vocation," 29.

the individuals, who compose the group, reveal in their personal relationships.[29]

Institutions do not have the morality that individuals have, but they exert a rational social force. But why do we need institutions in the first place? As Walter Wink says, "Without institutionalization, ideas never materialize into action. Institutions are indispensable for human existence, and they have a right to be concerned about their own survival. But they must keep this concern penultimate, not ultimate."[30] Moltmann also affirms that "every political power contains an element of 'good order' without which there can be no common human life. Civil authority is created by God and equipped with a monopoly of force so that social peace might be preserved and political justice established."[31] But since power tends to corrupt, institutions also incline toward groups of vested interests. Exclusive and unjust policies are "a collective egoism" compounded by individual sin. Knowing this does not annul social sin, but rather warns human beings of the even more precariousness of social sin.

What, then, are the social and institutional dimensions of sin? Primarily, individual decisions may be locked into social structures of injustice (like policies and laws) that oppress human beings, violate human dignity and aggravate existing inequality. Secondly, individual acts may foster social occasions (like campaigns and movements) that promote the well-being of one subgroup at the expense of another group. These preferential or discriminatory social actions are extensions of human selfishness. Thirdly, when a growing number of individuals do not take responsibility for the evil being done to others, it will give rise to a social norm of acquiescence to large-scale injustice. The mechanism to correct wrongs in social structures is switched off by such silencing of the individual conscience, a social sin of omission. Fourthly, when the privileged group gains dominance in establishing these institutions

---

29. Niebuhr, *Moral Man and Immoral Society*, xi–xii.
30. Wink, *Engaging the Powers*, 66.
31. Moltmann, *On Human Dignity*, 116.

and ideologies, the latter, in turn, foster a "false consciousness" that convinces the public that these actions are in fact good and beneficial for society. As Mark O'Keefe illustrates, "a welfare system which subtly penalizes or demeans the poor, tax systems that allow individual citizens to preserve their privileges at the expense of the poor, and silent acceptance of international trade and monetary systems which injure third world nations are all examples of social sin at work."[32] The tragic incidents described in the beginning of this book raise questions concerning the human cost of economic development and human dignity.

If human language at the policy level distorts truth and fairness, it is only the beginning of creating a climate for national disasters. For example, by naming distorting policies for agricultural output as "scissors' price," the Chinese mindset of communist planning created in its language a normative way to parade evil as instrumental. It was this twist of the market price mechanism that placed millions of peasants at economic disadvantage. Economists who served as counselors to the communist regime not only performed sins of omission, they also actively helped to build injustice into the economic institutions. The derogatory and categorical language of the *hukou* system in China serves an example. By creating an inherited rural category and identity, it created the dynamics of a downward spiral for peasants whose "agricultural" category was passed on to their later generations until today.

Such institutionalized evil then evolved historically and led to the poverty of generations of people. At a more informal level, the harm of this institutionalized evil lies in the fact that it creates a discriminatory attitude toward peasantry. In China, this has always been a prevailing social attitude. Rural peasants and migrant workers suffer from a prolonged collective stigmatization. Their disadvantaged self-identity has become quasi-ethnic. For example, marriages between urban and rural *hukou*-holders would always encounter immense difficulties, sometimes like inter-racial tension. By these social norms, communal cohesiveness is undermined. The society is gradually molded into "a chain

32. O'Keefe, *What Are They Saying*, 29.

of contempt" or "a pecking order" that is dominated by privileges and despising the powerless. Here the prophecy of social Darwinism finds fulfillment.

Worse still, an inherited status of inferiority makes systemic evil a reality that can be inherited. All economic systems, whether capitalist or communist, share the same tendency toward inequality, but the central-planning system has a built-in propensity to produce even graver outcomes. The irony lies in their futile attempts to erase class differences by first identifying and categorizing people into different classes. Although communist revolutions normally aim at changing existing power structures, its approach proves to be self-defeating.

In human groups, with different natural endowments, patterns of inequality emerge. Some are due to injustice, but some are not. So, the problem is still seeking unity in the midst of diversity. Ironically, Communist planning truncates such unity-seeking by putting individuals into rigid grids. It works against the organic processes of human solidarity.

As economic historian Karl Polanyi points out, understanding the problem of evil in this world is incomplete without a notion of social sin. In this respect, Catholic theologians are doing a better job, compared to Protestants' splintering theologies and fragmented worldview(s). Most of the latter would have difficulty thinking of institutions as moral agencies that may sin. Reformed protestants probably are placed in a more advantageous place of having a biblical worldview with the tutelage of Abraham Kuyper, Herman Dooyeweerd, and a few others. They acknowledge the dynamic interconnection between the personal dimension of sin and its social dimensions, because as sociologists Peter Berger and Thomas Luckman says, "Society is a human product.... Man is a social product."[33] As Walter Wink insightfully put it, "Institutions have an actual spiritual ethos, and we neglect this aspect of institutional life to our peril."[34]

---

33. Berger and Luckmann, *Social Construction of Reality*, 79.
34. Wink, *Engaging the Powers*, 6.

3

Urbanism and Alienation

> The city is not just a collection of ramparts with houses, but also a spiritual power... It is capable of directing and changing one's spiritual life. It brings its power to bear in one and changes one's life.
>
> —Jacques Ellul

CHINA'S URBANIZATION BEGAN ONLY "a while ago," according to Friedmann, who termed it as "hyper-urbanization."[1] A comparison with other Western countries shows that, in China, this process lagged 150 to 200 years behind the growth of an urban population in Europe and North America.[2] Though delayed, its scale has been mind-boggling. For example, since 2000, China alone has used nearly half the world's cement supplies to form urban infrastructure. More than a hundred cities now have a population exceeding one million, a number unparalleled in the world. After almost two decades of a thriving housing market, today's China is leading a global "new urbanism" through swift and radical commodification of urban space.[3] But behind the glamorous façade of urban prosperity, millions of rural migrants and their families have borne the costly alienation of a system combining the dual forces of socialism and capitalism.

Socialist collectivization instituted a bifurcation of the countryside and the city in China, as members of rural and urban collectives lived and worked in mutually exclusive domains.

1. Friedmann, "Four Theses," 440.
2. Friedmann, "Four Theses," 442.
3. Wu, *China's Emerging Cities*, 16.

For example, marriage between individuals who belonged to different categories was rare throughout the collectivist era. As the basic institution for procurement and redistribution of food and necessities, *hukou* gradually became a status hierarchy, a system of social distinction. Recently, China's market transition, beginning in 1978, ended peasants' serf-like ties to Maoist village communes. With *en masse* migration to cities, the typical rural family has adopted a "one household, two systems" model; that is, some family members (usually women, children, and the elderly) stay put, while a few others venture into the city for jobs.

Urban Construction in China (photo taken by the author)

Escaping Socialist Shackles

Market transition brought about multiple venues for peasants' mobility: employment, marriage, and education. As social interactions between rural and urban dwellers increased, intermarriage between the two social groups became less rare and was admired as a means of upward mobility. College education offered an even more efficient stepping stone for the better-educated peasants to "jump over the rural-urban threshold" (*tiao nongmen*). The previous caste-like system strictly separating the peasantry from the working class seemed to be breaking down, though not entirely. A report in 2003 shows that rural migrants composed 57 percent of the manufacturing sector, 80 percent of the construction sector, and over 50 percent of the service sector.[4] These rural migrants have powered China's soaring economy—it is estimated that rural migrants have contributed to 21 percent of China's GDP growth since the reform.[5] While the old working class—urban workers—is being dismantled in the state sector due to massive layoffs in the mid-1990s, rural migrants formed a substitute working class in the booming urban economy.

Meanwhile, reality also presents another side of the story—to break with the inherited identity of "peasants" remains a formidable goal, especially under a reform that is gradualist in nature and continues to be governed by *hukou*. In Shanghai, for example, formal legislative barriers channeled rural migrants to unskilled jobs in industries such as manufacturing (25.8 percent), construction (19.6 percent), trade (13.9 percent), agriculture (7.3 percent), delivery services (6.9 percent), catering services (6.6 percent), and others.[6] Only 3.8 percent were employed as skilled workers.

During my interviews with rural migrants, whenever they showed a pessimistic attitude about these remnant discriminatory practices, they tended to rationalize it. Many expressed an understanding tone of the system's difficulties by saying, "If everyone could come to Shanghai and settle down here, what would become of the city?" Their logic is closely aligned with official rhetoric. They would then comment that the urban and rural disparity just seems too large to be mended overnight for a country as populous as China. To call this injustice does not occur to these migrants. They have internalized systemic oppression.

Most solo migrants endure the hardships of work in the city with the hope that their children might attend urban schools someday in the future. But toward the late 1990s, this hope has

4. "Migrant Labor," 16.
5. Cai and Wang, "Sustainability of China's Economic Growth," 62–88.
6. "Shanghai 2000 Population Census."

been shattered by exclusive rules in urban schools that reject children of rural origin. Even for those able to pay extra fees or bribe officials to get their children enrolled, within a few years they face the stark reality of being denied the opportunity to take key-point exams in the city for continued schooling. It is often when they hit this ceiling of educational mobility that many expressed outrage against systemic unfairness.

When I first interviewed Qin (forty), he had been working at H district's Engineering Inspection Bureau (EIB), a public *danwei* (work unit), for over eleven years. Despite his high seniority among his colleagues, Qin has been referred to as the "temporary staff." Being one of the two rural-status workers in this *danwei*, Qin belongs to the tiny fraction of rural migrants working in professional career tracks. Wearing a blue technician uniform in his own office, Qin looks like any other experienced engineer. When asked how he likes this job, Qin says contently, "Now I have freed myself from manual jobs, so that counts as an improvement." His routine tasks require only technical inspections of ongoing construction projects in H district. To Qin, a promotion to formal status sounds untenable for him—"It is already such a privilege to be able to work here!" he says. Working as a member of this formal *danwei* is already a dream job for him.

Growing up as a country boy, Qin never saw the city until he reached the age of twenty-four. He came with some relatives to work in the construction industry in eastern Shanghai. He started the job in 1992, and for more than five years Qin worked twelve hours a day, seven days a week. His brother Yuan later entered a prestigious university in Shanghai, and Qin supported his tuition expenses. By 1995, Yuan was about to graduate with academic excellence and a college degree in engineering. It was a time when college graduates still enjoyed job allocations by the state, and engineers were highly desired by many research institutes. Yuan was assigned to be an engineer. He was among the few graduates with rural-*hukou* to land on such jobs. After one year of work, Yuan turned in a request for a personal assistant, which created a temporary position for his brother. That was how

Qin first obtained his current job. He later turned out to be a good fit for the tasks assigned to him, so this temporary worker stayed for the next eleven years.

Despite his seniority, Qin's rural *hukou* status made him unqualified to be listed as formal personnel according to legal regulations. Thus, Qin receives a much lower stipend on top of a minimum wage (840 yuan in 2007). With his wife working at a wool factory, the couple makes around 3000 yuan per month in 2008, an upper-middle level income among rural migrant families in Shanghai. Qin kept telling me, "It's so much better than when we first came to Shanghai."

A decent job, a stable income and a family all together are probably the dream for many rural migrants. Qin seems to have it all, but life still has its frustrations. A major worry is his son's education. Surprisingly, the fifteen-year-old boy is still in Fifth Grade, while most of his classmates are eleven or twelve years old. Qin explains, "When the [migrant] schools he entered either moved or closed down, we had to transfer him several times. Every time the new school just required him to re-take first grade. So, he has taken first-grade classes three times."

Like most rural migrant families, Qin is also greatly worried about where to send his son for secondary education. "If he has to return [to the countryside] for middle school, then my wife probably will go back with him. I'll stay here by myself. But I think I'll return home sooner or later." Qin wishes to save around 100 thousand yuan to start up a small business at home, maybe a chicken farm or a farm machinery rental shop. Many migrants like Qin have returned and started small businesses in the towns near their native villages. Opportunities abound there too.

The nature of partial reform dictates that China's economic structures remain bound by rules and legacies inherited from its old redistributive framework. Rural migrant workers are an indispensable but an easily replaceable labor force. The Chinese state reaps fame for its economic miracle, but this massive invisible labor force bears the pains of distorted labor prices and unjust treatment.

Despite these structural difficulties, self-made migrant businesses of all kinds have flourished, gradually forming into sizable informal economic enclaves. Many self-organized small-scale operations are based on shared provincial origins, such as in garment-manufacturing (Zhejiang), restaurants (Hunan, Sichuan), renovation (Anhui), recycling (Henan), doorstep delivery (Jiangsu), etc. For almost three decades, the growing "grey zone" of China's informal economy has offered both opportunities for migrant entrepreneurship and a buffer for migrants' survival. But, over time, with roadblocks to upward mobility for the younger migrants, they will be unable to escape the fate of continued marginalization and their vulnerability to economic downturns.

Serving Capitalist Mammons

When rural migrants themselves refer to their work in the city, the word *dagong* is used most frequently.[7] It literally means sporadic employment, working "informally" or "irregularly" for a boss. It is a state of work which differs from being affiliated with any work unit, entailing irregular work, unregistered status, high job mobility, income insecurity, residential instability and, most of the time, arduous manual labor. Rural migrants set up a categorical contrast between *dagong* jobs from "doing business." The latter is much desired because it promises being one's own boss and enjoying more freedom. For many of them, *dagong* for "some boss" delivers negative "capitalist" connotations for a rural Chinese who still cling to a political consciousness in the socialist era. In the pursuit of economic gains in the urban society at large, many rural migrants feel at a loss when relationships and careers are often commodified in purely materialistic terms.

Rural migrants' desire for economic autonomy through self-employment is driven not only by such ideological nostalgia and over reliance on networks, but also by the blocked opportunities and lack of cultural identification in the city. Take rural migrants

---

7. This kind of work is akin to temporary workers in the United States, but with no benefits or security.

from Henan, for example. The widespread social prejudice against Henan migrants, who are depicted as lazy and prone-to-theft, has contributed to the group's overrepresentation in the recycling sector. In suburban Beijing, many villages containing migrants from Henan have been turned into "trash villages." There are clusters of recyclers who came from the same rural locality, such as Gushi in Henan province.

Many other small businesses (such as street vending, repair, restaurant, shops) are established to serve fellow migrants in their concentrated neighborhoods. They offer affordable foods or grocery items at cheaper prices than other places. My NGO friends and I always enjoyed spending only sixteen yuan on three nice dishes at a small Sichuan diner inside a rural migrant community, which may be priced at over sixty yuan in another main street Sichuan restaurant. These businesses also attract many students from nearby college campuses and low-income urban workers from adjacent factories.

The emergence of these job opportunities is also closely linked with public policy changes in the city. Take street vending, for instance. It was not until 2006 when the Shanghai government issued policies endorsing "informal employment" in its economy. Before then, street vendors led a "guerrilla" lifestyle. Conflicts between street venders and urban administrators (*chengguan*) abounded in major cities. After the city government of Shanghai relaxed its "street code" against such vending in 2006, these workers are now more at peace, although haphazard confiscations still occasionally occur. Some street committees (the urban grassroots-level government organ) even actively rebuild and rent out spaces for migrant businesses in their neighborhoods.

In some regions, small businesses are less protected, and the presence of public authorities is more visible and dominating. Here, grassroots administrators "loosely" cooperated in facilitating market activities, so "unlicensed" migrant businesses continue to be viewed with suspicion. Registration is still used as the tool for governance.

A migrant worker's locksmith shop (courtesy of Joann Pittman)

Some migrant entrepreneurs who can venture into more formal markets are faced with high rental prices, minimum earnings requirements and fee collection for this or that reason. In some neighborhoods, street committees collude with the Bureau of Industry and Commerce in creating formidable rules for open rent seeking.

Rural migrants consider sporadic employment a norm in the city, so joblessness is not in their vocabulary. One either finds some casual work to do for today, or none. The latter is not considered unusual. This is because, to them, most accessible jobs are already outside the formal employment category. Jobs in certain formal *danwei* are out of their reach, because those spots are reserved for urban residents, according to the long socialist tradition. Although times have changed, they still hold onto a type of undeserving mindset in the way they evaluate career choices. So, the most typical jobs held by rural migrants include those shunned by urban residents: construction work, suburban factory jobs, domestic service, providing security, and restaurant work. Every sector has its distinctiveness in terms of economic opportunities and structural hurdles.

Rural migrants in manufacturing often face the risk of overwork and stage suicide protests against sweatshop-like conditions. But in the construction industry, the risk of no-payment at all is much higher. Such jobs are considered entry-level work for most solo male migrants, since lodging and food are provided. Almost all the males I interviewed had taken up construction jobs at some points in their city life, but very few stuck with this job for very long. Construction is hard, backbreaking work, and most construction workers are required to work twelve hours per day, seven days a week. The All China Federation of Trade Unions (ACFTU) recently announced that, according to the Fifth PRC Population Census, over eighty percent of workers in the construction sector are rural migrants.

Liu, a forty-year-old man from rural Anhui, had worked in Shanghai's rising Pudong area since 1992. The work left him proud memories as a contributor to a page-turning moment for the new Shanghai. He first followed his relatives to the city and started as a casual laborer with the construction team. The low pay was based on piecework, where 6.5 yuan was paid per piece, and each piece took about eight hours to complete. However, Liu enjoyed studying the machine manuals when he was off shift. Liu worked and learned to operate the machines for a year; then he decided that his body could not take it anymore. Seeing a co-worker badly injured by a machine and then dismissed with scant compensation, Liu determined to leave for other safer jobs.

Migrant workers like Liu have experienced and contributed to a world-class project—China's unrivaled urbanization since the 1990s. From 1992 to 1994, Shanghai's new Pudong area, for example, has attracted foreign investment that has grown from $3.5 billion to $10 billion in just two years, pumping up the "largest construction project the planet has ever seen."[8] But the product of their labor is alienated from the credit (even in monetary terms) that is attributed to them. Who could have thought that the Marxist idea of alienation is best realized in the lives of these

---

8. Sterba, "Great Leap," para. 9.

rural migrants in a communist state that upholds Marxist ideals? The irony is striking.

Construction workers are a highly homogeneous group, mostly young adults of twenty to forty years of age, less educated, single or without dependents, living in cramped and poorly built temporary dorms on construction sites. They are often recruited by "migrant contractors" (*bao gongtou*), who have worked in the cities long enough to have accumulated wide personal connections. This industry has become the most notorious for abusing rural migrant workers. There are many reasons. First, very few rural migrants establish a protected labor contract with their employers. Second, the organizational structure overseeing a construction project is often so complicated that it's beyond a rural migrant's knowledge to fulfill the due responsibilities. Over-reliance on native-place networks surrender rural migrants to the willful manipulation of contractors that they trust. As a result, wage arrears are frequent. Statistics from the Ministry of Construction show that in 2003, the construction industry alone owed rural migrants 3.2 million yuan in total (roughly four hundred thousand United States dollars). Considering the low wages these migrants usually earn, one could imagine the scale of such labor abuse must be colossal. In the spring of 2003, the public media in China cast unusual attention upon the plight of migrant workers in this sector. Wage delays and arrears peaked in that year, causing widespread discontent and climatic cases of "suicidal appeals" by rural migrants. The situation became so serious that the new leadership put this issue at the top of its agenda in the government report at the Annual Meeting of the People's Congress in 2004.

The temporary nature of construction jobs also increased rural migrants' vulnerability to external changes, making them an expendable labor force in times of political sensitivity. The presence of more than six million rural migrants in Beijing before the Olympics became a very sensitive issue during my fieldwork. On September 14, 2008, the city's Olympic Legislation and Coordination Committee publicized measures to regulate the rural migrant population by "encouraging" them to return home. Construction companies were urged to change their hiring policies in hiring rural migrants, cutting the number by one million. Although this information was released the next day on the People's Congress news update, many officials denied the enactment of this policy two weeks later when foreign reporters inquired about it. The city's new policies also required incoming rural migrants to obtain county-level and above certificates for finding jobs in Beijing. Most of the builders of the Bird's Nest stadium and other Olympic venues had to "disappear" during the clean-up campaign prior to the Games. My field trips in July and October confirmed the reality of mass return migration through abandoned construction projects and migrant schools within Beijing's Fifth ring.

With China's real estate market booming, the need for manual labor has been increasing in the area of construction and renovation. Renovation jobs are often taken by experienced migrant workers who have worked as contractors. Usually six or seven veteran migrant workers can form a renovation team. They sometimes find work through personal networks, or they simply wait in the informal renovation marketplace for clients to find them.

Trust and network building are two important components for success in this industry. Rural migrants in this sector also split into smaller locality-based networks with occupational prestige for trustworthiness. In Shanghai, the majority of jobs are taken by Anhui natives despite their reputation of low trustworthiness among urban clients.

The fact that trust plays a sensitive building block in the organization of this sector is important to understand. Since the entry level skills for renovation work is very low, any group of semi-skilled workers could hastily start an informal "guerrilla renovation company." Some low-quality teams use price competition to weed out others. Even some registered formal renovation companies sub-contract their projects to "guerrilla renovation teams" to cut costs. Moreover, cheating on material costs is widespread. Some workers over-report the amount of wood or tiles that are needed, and hoard these extra materials as profit. These "guerrilla" renovation teams have closely collaborated with material providers in the marketplace. Often, kickback payments are expected for securing a deal. These processes all contributed to the "chaotic" and trust-sensitive features of the renovation industry.

Factory jobs in the manufacturing industry have attracted millions of female migrants to the cities. Only a decade ago, rural migrants were not allowed to work in state and foreign enterprises. Now these factories have adopted outsourcing or informalized hiring strategies to reduce labor costs. They are not legally bound to provide insurance or other benefits to rural migrants. These so-called advantages contributed to the "China Price."

Free meals and dormitories are attractive to many female migrants. Jobs like these seem to provide basic stability and a relatively protected environment from hazardous encounters in the city. But factory dorms are not cozy havens for individual fulfillment; rather, they have been called highly "segregative regimes," resembling a "mini-paternalistic state."[9] Work is highly routinized and rigidly enforced. In South China, over 80 percent of assembly-line workers are female rural migrants who are subject to this type of workplace regime. Apart from long working hours, workers are constantly under strict surveillance by video cameras or watchful managers. Their bodily postures are tamed under specific terms of control. Sometimes factory owners and managers deliberately paint a picture of the "insecure outside world" to migrant workers, bolstering the legitimacy of this man-made segregative regime. Factory leaders use big printed slogans like "Love the Factory as My Home" to encourage greater loyalty and commitment from workers. Contrary to my expectations, I found in my fieldwork interviews that working overtime was rarely the cause for complaints. Some of my informants actually preferred to enter into factories with "opportunities for overtime work," because that way they could earn more money in a shorter time. When some factories have fewer orders coming in, a portion of workers decide to quit because "there's no overtime work."

On their payrolls, rural migrant workers are classified as "labor workers" in contrast to urban workers, who are known

---

9. Lee, *Against the Law*; Lu and Hunt, "Photographer Captures."

as "contractual workers." These terms are intended to give a certain legitimacy to China's "equal work, unequal pay" policies. Second-generation rural migrants have grown more sensitive to status inequalities than their parents' generation. Twenty-two-year-old Lan is a second-generation migrant of rural Henan origin. In the early 1990s, after a big flood wiped out their crops, her parents packed all their belongings onto a tractor and drove one week until they reached suburban Shanghai. Now Lan works in an electronics manufacturing factory, where she uses machines that test the quality of chips. She showed me some pictures in which she is dressed in a blue uniform and operating machines in a high-tech workplace. The job does not involve many skills, according to Lan, "just pressing buttons and watching over some indicators on the screen."

Lan is well aware of the wage differences between local workers and migrant workers. Although she never lived in rural regions herself and thus is not a migrant in the truest sense, her *hukou* status states otherwise. Lan can operate the machine better than her urban peers, but in a *hukou*-segregated system, she is not entitled to equal benefits or promotional opportunities that others receive. Her parents were indebted to the factory for taking their daughter in, but according to Lan, the payment policy was a stark inequality from the beginning: "Local workers enjoy three types of insurance. And their wage is twice as high as ours. We are paid thirty a day, they get sixty, but we do the same work! It is simply unfair!"

Factories in Shanghai's suburban districts resemble southern cities such as Guangdong and Shenzhen. Their assembly lines attract thousands of girls in their late teens and early twenties, mostly newcomers to the city. Those who have worked for years develop a pattern of job-hopping from one factory to another, seeking better pay or better work conditions. Most of them eventually found that all these factories offer almost the same: arduous long hours, strict restrictions against talking, limited bathroom breaks, poor meals and overcrowded dorms.

It is not unusual to see graduates from low-tiered colleges working side-by-side on the assembly line with semi-illiterate village girls who just stepped out of mountainous Sichuan. Manufacturing has attracted mostly single male and female graduates from secondary or higher education institutes. For young people from many poor rural families, failing the national college entrance exam simply means that they must leave home to find jobs in the cities. Some better-off rural families rush to enroll their children into fourth-tier or fifth-tier private colleges that charge ridiculous tuitions, some amounting to 200,000 yuan per year. But graduates from these low-quality colleges later prove to be uncompetitive in the labor market.

Compared with factory jobs, life as a live-in domestic helper promises an easier workload for women. As early as the beginning of 1980s, live-in maids made the first wave of rural-urban migration into cities. Young and nimble girls from rural areas created a niche market and became a sought-after brand for domestic services. Later, as this market differentiated, female migrants from different regions were labeled according to different traits and qualities of service for middle-class urban families to choose from. These young girls, often in their late teens, catered not only to the daily routines of the families, but also functioned as a status symbol for households that had them. Having a live-in maid to take care of household chores became a status necessity for many urban elite families.

The experiences of a live-in maid present a study in contrast. A strong status hierarchy sets up an unbridgeable chasm between the maid and her employer. However, the maid is closely involved in the most private matters of the household, such as taking care of the children or the elderly, and other daily chores. As the intimate stranger in the urban family, this job also comes with emotional stress as her role can emerge as a deeply problematic one, both indispensable to the smooth running of the household and yet threatening her employer's privacy. Stories of sexual abuse by employers or revenge by maids are not a rarity.

Survey results show that because legal protection is lacking, the pool of domestic maids in many cities is shrinking. Xinhua News reported in early 2007 that in Beijing alone, the market for domestic helpers has more than 100,000 unfilled posts. Some urban residential areas have started to organize collective searches for domestic maids through personal networks. Some domestic jobs, such as caring for nursing new mothers, saw salaries rocket to 10,000 yuan a month by 2010.

Having worked for seven years as a security guard for Cultural Garden, a high-end residential community in central Shanghai, twenty-six-year-old Hong has now been promoted as the "foreman" (*banzhang*) of sixty security guards. The work schedule is based on three shifts per day, in turn, around the clock, with the main duties of registering incoming visitors and checking every corner of their assigned areas for potential dangers. Hong says that worker turnover is very high, because most young people leave for other jobs after several months. "After all, it's 'a job requiring young age' (*qingchunfan*), meaning that you cannot work at it forever."

To rural migrants, a job in the security field exposes them to the most manifested "relative deprivation" in the city. In some gated luxury residential communities, they see the most extravagant expressions of urban consumerism and overt discrimination against their "ruralness." Without any systematic legal protection for their rights, exploitation in the form of suppressed or withheld income tends to lead to eruptions of envy and hatred. Hate crimes between the gated class and the guards have been reported. For example, *Beijing News* reported a murder on December 9, 2007, that alerted all city dwellers to the hidden pathologies behind these gated communities. The convict was twenty-three years old, 160 cm tall and frail-looking by the name of Zheng, who had worked as a security guard for this residential area for one year. For his meager wage of 700 yuan per month, he had to work daily eight-hour shifts, sometimes overtime for another two yuan per hour. Like other young guards, Zheng seldom had time or money for sightseeing or recreation. Months of social isolation and discriminatory attitudes from the residents in this community eventually led to an eruption of emotions on the part of Zheng, when he was humiliated and beaten by a local young man for the eighth time. After this abuse, all guards in Zheng's team reported similar mistreatments and simultaneously quit their jobs. This incident exposed the living conditions of young migrants who work in these positions, and the prevalence of urban discrimination against these temporary workers.

A rural migrant who works as a recycler is easy to identify—he or she rides an empty tricycle cart with plastic ropes in it, ringing a bell when riding along the street. While doing this, most recyclers invent their own long, rhythmic "tunes" to remind familiar clients that they are passing by the urban communities. A recycler often has his or her "territory" to keep, often a gated residential community or compound. He or she parks the cart at the side of the road, adjacent to the gate but not intrusively close to it. Some security guards may come up and inquire about him or her, if this is a new recycler in the neighborhood. But usually that works out all right, if the territory has not already been claimed. Residents of that community get used to the recycler's presence every day, and within a week a client network takes form in that area.

Migrant recyclers (courtesy of Joann Pittman)

Getting to know what it is like to work as a recycler, or the more demeaning term "trash collector," is no easy task. It took me over a year to build trust among the Zhang family so that they would be comfortable talking about what they do every day. They have been recyclers in Shanghai for eight years. The first time I asked about what they did for living, they just shyly shunned it as "nothing to talk about." Like many jobs taken by rural migrants, recyclers provide a necessity service to urban residents, but the nature of their job adds a shadow to their collective self-identity.

Later, I learned more about the couple's daily routine: after making breakfast and sending their three children to school around 7:30 every morning, the Zhangs ride their cart along the riverbank all the way to a more central district. The ride usually takes two hours one-way, and they collect trash and purchase used items along the way. This route takes them past an industrial zone with many gated factories and then some wealthy residential compounds. They return home around 1 or 2 p.m. for lunch, then take a short nap. Another ride starts from 4 p.m., following a different one-hour route. Then they come back around 6 p.m. to wait for their children and make dinner.

Mr. Zhang did not work as a recycler when he first left the countryside. That was in the late 1980s, and the city was Beijing. He took a job selling mushrooms by bike around Beijing's maze of *hutongs* (historic alleys). He still takes pride in the fact that he used to know all the *hutongs* of Beijing. Later, he worked on construction sites for a few more years. Although the pay was only a little above 100 yuan per month, that was already about one fifth of the annual income for an average rural peasant in 1989. Between 1989 and 1994, he returned home every year during harvest and later got married. Remaining there, they bore one daughter and two sons. They were heavily fined for violating the one-child policy. The financial penalty for flouting the policy varied from region to region, but Zhang's hometown was especially strict with peasants for this offence. They incurred 20,000 yuan in debt, about four years of income for a rural household in the early 1990s. This debt became the direct cause for the couple to leave for city jobs.

During one of my last visits to their community one day, I found the Zhangs idling at home. It was the beginning of a recession when the prices of raw materials dropped sharply, so most mobile recyclers in the cities lost their businesses. Only large-scale recycling centers survived. The family's monthly income dropped to one third of its regular level. A week later, the recycling business had not recovered. I called to ask what their plans might be. Returning home was not an option to them because the three children were still in the middle of their academic semesters. Mrs. Zhang later found another job as the cleaning lady for a night bar kitchen, from 7 p.m. to 12 p.m. every night. The time was inconvenient, but the pay was good: 1000 yuan per month. Mr. Zhang makes his usual ride every day, sometimes making ten to twenty yuan a day. This was good enough to buy some food for the family. In the end, they had to stay and find whatever jobs they could, until their oldest son finished seventh grade.

Rootlessness

China's official labor statistics count as unemployed only those who register for unemployment benefits with local governments. Therefore, these numbers are widely believed to understate the true economic picture, since the two hundred million rural migrants are left out of most surveys or census sampling frames. Unemployment haunts not only new arrivals but also long-term settlers in the city. During my ten-month fieldwork in Shanghai, two major structural changes affected the job situations of rural migrants most acutely. The first was the revision and enactment of the new Labor and Contract Law (which took effect from Jan 1, 2008), which drastically changed employers' hiring practices. The new law, from its onset, sought to protect workers' rights by making contractual relationships binding on employers. It also increased the cost to employers for arbitrary dismissal of workers. It is stipulated that an employer that breaches a contractual relationship must pay six months of wages to the worker as compensation.

The second change was that the announcement of this legislation was followed by *en masse* layoffs before it was implemented. Towards the end of 2007, more and more private enterprises reacted to this policy change by innovating ways to avoid the risks: layoffs, relocation, creating a separate category according to the "labor dispatchment" (*laodong paiqian*) policy to outsource workers. Because many factories did not have management systems in place to operate in accordance with the new law, some were simply noncompliant.

The new labor law triggered a hidden crisis that had long been fermented by multiple causes over the previous few years, such as rising raw material costs and China's appreciating currency. Large-scale layoffs happened across major manufacturing cities. In Dongguan, the most flourishing manufacturing zone in Guandong province, 20 to 30 percent of shoe factories closed, according to the Asian Shoes Industry Association (ASIA).

Public media started discussions about the precarious situation for over twenty million jobless rural migrants since February of 2009, with titles like "Should Jobless Rural Migrants Stay or Return?" Given this unprecedented scale of unemployment, "social stability" once again mounted as the state's biggest worry. This familiar rhetoric had a long history, as rural migrants have always been considered a threat to public order. With more and more workers increasingly aware of their rights and with labor-related lawsuits rising by 95 percent in 2008, the government braced for the likelihood that this group would eagerly claim its rights. However, among rural migrants who had lost their jobs, very few expressed dissatisfaction with the authorities. The public media did a good job of attributing unemployment to a global economic crisis, something beyond the control of the Chinese state.

During this time, rural migrants' access to basic social security (such as unemployment insurance) also came into the spotlight. Although the state promised and designed pension schemes for rural migrants, the reality fell short of these plans. Since job mobility is so high for rural migrants, it's hard for them to settle in one location for a long time. Thus, the legal stipulations that require pensioners to have paid fifteen years of premiums in one location and that pension accounts cannot be transferred to a new workplace or to their rural hometowns puts migrants in real jeopardy. Social insurance benefits are not "portable" when they move. Some workers, fearing they will not be able to recoup their contributions, do not even bother to pay into the scheme. According to state media reports, of the small fraction (about 15 percent of the total migrant labor force) who did pay dues, over 95 percent chose to cash in (*tuibao*) their contribution. Since they are being left out of the formal employment and social insurance system, rural migrants live like undocumented immigrants in their own country, and are thereby more vulnerable during times of illness, unemployment or aging.

Similar public welfare failures demonstrate that social security policy makers have not taken rural migrants' interests into consideration. In Shenzhen, for example, rural migrants are eligible to draw a retirement pension once they have contributed to the city's fund for fifteen years and have reached the mandated retirement age (fifty for women, sixty for men). But very few rural migrants would meet these conditions. For aging rural migrants, retiring in the city is virtually unimaginable given the rising living costs and slim job opportunities. Most middle-aged respondents that I interviewed anticipated returning to their small patches of land in the countryside.

Nowadays, rural China is gradually seeing its villages "growing grey" with more and more senior citizens. Rural migrants exchange their youth for living in the city, but when they grow old and dependent, there is no mechanism to protect their benefits. First generation migrants willingly return to the land with their memories and emotional attachments, but for second-generation migrants, going back to the villages is not even an option. Mei (forty, female) has been an NGO worker helping rural schools for over two decades. She observes a downward spiral of poverty and despair in many rural areas of China:

> Many phenomena are worsening nowadays. For example, rural schools are depleted with good spirit. Teachers lack skills and responsibility. Children who stayed in rural villages either live with the elderly or enroll in boarding schools. It disheartens me to see them bearing

the negative consequences of the whole society—eating unhealthy food, not medically informed to take the right medications when sick, feeding their minds with a lot of TV-watching. They don't have real childhoods. No emotional attachments to anyone, but only empty minds and fearful hearts. All the adults and teachers kept telling them that if they do not achieve better in school, then they would be thrown into a very dark society with no way out.

By 2017, the first generation of rural migrants who ventured out to China's cities have grown old, but without any social welfare to support them. Meng, forty-two, a migrant-turned-NGO-staff, told me that her biggest wish was to set up a nursing home which accepts and cares for senior migrants in the city. "It took us two to three generations to make such a prosperous city," Meng says. "Why are migrants not allowed to stay when they get old?" Indeed, Meng's question points out the core of the problem—rural peasants are now allowed to freely move and work, but the choice to stay in the city is still beyond their reach.

Being a rural migrant who commutes between one's home village and the host city is a hybrid experience that challenges one's sense of self and belonging. The lack of formal rights deprives rural migrants of expectations for material and symbolic equality. Their vulnerable positions at the fringes of the urban economy, coupled with widespread exploitation at workplaces, often shatter even their dimmest expectations. Many rural migrants had to return to home villages during joblessness, work injuries, or other social traumas while in the city. In early 2009, the economic downturn sent millions of rural migrants back to their villages due to job loss. Months after the massive return, social problems intensified in rural areas, including land disputes and crime. Some young people became jaded with boredom at home and ventured out again for new opportunities. An informant told me, "When I idled in the city without a job, I felt so homeless; but when I went back to my home village, the longer I stayed, the more I hated it. I grew restless, so I had to come out again."

A rural home in China (photo taken by the author)

Searching for a sense of "home" between the soil and the city, rural migrants live in a constant state of "transience." Such is the experience of Kang. Once again, Kang comes back to this oddly familiar urban neighborhood. He realizes that he needs to start all over again: finding a place to live, a job, and a life to get by, as a stranger in this city. To save some money, this time he decides to share a single room with a young man he just met who is also looking for a job in the nearby food and electronics factories. After getting some daily necessities, Kang starts making inquiries into the over twenty informal job centers there. These information centers usually place big chalk boards outside with information about jobs in these factories. But for the most up-to-date information, one is required to pay 30 percent of the indicated wage, as a commission fee for the job center to contact the factories. These job centers are opened by migrants themselves who are better connected with local businesses.

A week earlier, Kang went to the food factory where he had once worked, wishing to get back to his former job as a food assembler. In 2006, he had worked there for more than a year, before his wife asked him to return home. At that time, the factory paid him over 1800 yuan a month. Kang liked it because it was good pay and familiar work. He was quite confident about getting the job again. After all, factories prefer returned workers because they are more "experienced" and "know the way of doing things there."

This food factory mainly produces partially cooked products, such as frozen fried chicken legs, for fast-food stores. Like many other factories, assembly lines jobs are dominated by rural migrants, and a few Shanghai natives fill the office staff positions. Kang is content except for one minor complaint. Although meals and dorms are freely provided, the food factory enforces a "food code": workers are given only vegetarian meals. I ask why, and Kang hesitantly says that because managers assume that most workers are "consuming" their half-cooked chicken legs while packaging them. I then ask if workers do actually "consume" these chicken legs. With some embarrassment, Kang replies, "With such light meals, who does not eat? . . . one has to watch out though, because there is a huge penalty for that." Of all the random rules made by factories I heard through these interviews, this one sounds funny but yet humiliating at the same time. The factory's food code actually induces a norm of stealing by its underfed assembly line workers.

Young as he is, Kang's twenty-seven years of life has let him taste despair and many frustrations. Kang left rural Jiangsu when he was only sixteen, a few days before finishing junior middle school. School never appealed to him since his village teachers were uninspired and boring. Besides, his family needed more hands to help with the crops.

Kang's parents divorced early, leaving an indelible impact on him. His father took up recycling as a sideline job apart from farming to support Kang and his younger sister. From an early age, Kang heard people joking about his father's occupation—*jianpolan* (trash-collector). "It does not sound good [decent], but many of our villagers make good money out of it," Kang explains to me. The low prestige is counterbalanced by the fast cash it offers.

In 1996, Kang made his first venture into the city of Nanjing. Unable to find other jobs, he used thirty yuan as "start-up capital" for his own recycling business. "Since all my folks work in this trade, it is most familiar to me," he explained. However, Kang's first entrepreneurial attempt lasted twenty days. Then he moved to the Northeast with a few of his relatives. Some of them had worked as contractors at construction sites there. They allowed him to work as *"xiaogong"* (minor labor). Meals and accommodation were provided on site and for free, although the quality was poor for both. Nevertheless, Kang was content to get a more "decent" and "manly" job. He said he liked "a job requiring physical strength"; it made him feel good about himself.

Like most construction jobs, Kang was paid once a year. The boss did not cheat them, so he stayed there for two years. The only thing he grew dissatisfied with was that his wage did not increase over this time. When a few folks learned that construction workers in Shangdong were being paid thirty yuan a day, they decisively left. The following few years consisted of constant job changes from one construction team to another, depending on the length of the building projects.

In 2002, Kang reached the age of getting married, according to the customs in rural Jiangsu. He returned and married a girl from a neighboring village. In rural China, marriage and house-building are life-cycle events for the average migrant returnee, and these celebrated goals help offset one's difficult existence in the city. For over a year, Kang stayed with his new wife and worked in recycling with his father. Wanting some change in his life, he started a business that involved more risk: recycling metal materials. Kang successfully secured a 200,000 yuan bank loan, and he made over eight thousand yuan in just a week. When everything seemed to be going the right direction, and the young man was getting excited about the future, he was visited one day by some cadres from the local industry and commerce bureau. It turned out that for recycling metal materials, one needed to apply for a permit.

This incident threw Kang into a large amount of debt—the 200,000 yuan start up loan he must now repay without a chance to recoup his investments. Since then, Kang's marriage also started to show signs of crisis. His wife grew increasingly dissatisfied with his business failures. After their daughter was born in mid-2003, Kang decided to travel solo to Shanghai for jobs. Like seven years before, he came to the city with just two hands.

Kang experienced the lowest point of his life in Nanjing. After he spent all his savings of 1000 yuan, he was left to sleep on the streets, without food for several days. Later, someone offered him a carwash job with food and dorm. This experience of hopelessness left Kang so emotionally distraught that he worked for just ten days, then left for home with the 200 yuan wage he earned.

For many rural migrants, the vicissitudes of life set their course into the unknown and unsettled. They long for the city, but while they are there all alone, they long to return home. Life goes on in a circle. It took only a few months for Kang to feel the impulse to come out for work again. This is how his new search for jobs started at the beginning again. Now his motivation to persevere in the city is to pay back the loan. He also holds onto another dream that one day he might bring his kindergarten-age daughter to attend one of Shanghai's schools.

Millions of young factory workers live a life like Kang's. To some, their despair can soon be assuaged through spending what they have saved on themselves and on relatives back home. Consumerism has become a defining characteristic, if not an ideology, in current Chinese society. As in many other economies that are facing recession, the Chinese state reminds individuals how important "consumer confidence" is for the national economy. Moreover, with the rise of nationalism, purchasing Chinese brand names is associated with a sense of national responsibility or symbol of loyalty. "Chinese people should consume Chinese products" was the catchphrase among the young. The consumptive behaviors of rural migrants, especially the younger generation, is an important topic. To some extent, the rise of modern consumerism has reinforced urban bias.

A Double Yoke

China's partial liberalization from a central planning economy has created a double yoke for rural migrants: old shackles of socialist peasantry identity and a rapacious profit-driven capitalist economy. Economists have discussed the damaging social impact of a dual labor market for migrant workers. The primary labor market represents jobs offering relatively high wages, good working conditions, potentials for advancement, and protective work rules; the latter comprises work situations with few of these advantages. Discrimination persists and is reinforced within this system, and if education for the second generation also presents unequal opportunities, poverty and inequality will become a downward spiral for migrant laborers.

My field interviews also show that rural migrants have low expectations for job placement and wages, given their much lower pre-migration rural income.[10] So new arrivals tend to take any job available to recoup transportation expenses and money spent in applying for various permits in the city. Paying a substantial "deposit" at a new workplace has become a common practice, which obliges the new migrants to endure even exploitative work conditions. Some unscrupulous employers even withhold a portion of workers' monthly wage, promising to pay it at the end of the year. Another practice to retain rural migrants is for employers to seize their documents, as another form of "security deposit." Without these documents, rural migrants cannot switch jobs even under intolerable circumstances.

Unable to bargain with the state-sanctioned rules of rural-urban division, most rural migrants "rationalize" the appropriateness of being part of the informal economy. Formal rules, social norms, and individual expectations together form an institutional barrier that has led to the internalization of status inferiority. Such internalized inferiority discourages rural migrants' economic

---

10. China's income ratio between urban and rural increased dramatically, from 2.36:1 in the year 1978, to 3.2:1 in 2000. By 2005, the real rural income per capita was only 39 percent of actual urban income per capita. See Xiaochao, "China Statistical Yearbook 2008."

aspirations and weakens their authority in making fair negotiations with private employers or urban administrators.

Recent genuine efforts that push toward redefining the citizenship of peasants have brought scant results. Admittedly, occupational restrictions on enterprises that hire rural migrants have become greatly relaxed, but most formal professional-track jobs are still inaccessible to rural migrants. The urban labor market, overall, continues to be highly segregated according to residence. For the sake of economic development, local governments did make efforts to eliminate some restrictions on hiring rural migrants. However, when local unemployment became worrisome, they would revert to the default position of exclusive policies.

Theological Reflections: Urbanism and Alienation

The experiences of rural migrants in Chinese cities are particularly grueling because their sense of in-between-ness is intensified by the dual processes of communist political suppression and capitalist economic domination. They are a disposable group to both systems that extract profits from their inferior status. They are embedded in both systems, but also barred from social relations in both. The result is a deeper dehumanizing force and misery, a heavier set of chains created by half freedom from socialism and half freedom in the market.

Displacement for any human leads to anxiety and reshapes one's self-identity. As authors of *A Promised Land, A Perilous Journey* describe, "The experience of learning street names, metro stations, fixed schedules, bus numbers, and such in the new country only increases the stress, anxiety, and suffering of migrants. . . . If migrants do not overcome such loss, they may fall prey to a type of ethnic fundamentalism or cultural absolutism."[11] Moreover, the urban context combines two layers of impersonalization—bureaucratization or rational planning and transient anonymity. As

---

11. Groody and Campese, *Promised Land*, xiv.

Weber describes, modern capitalism is born with the tendency to render human relationships impersonal. Durkeim's theory of social transformation from mechanic solidarity to organic solidarity highlights the same thing. In contrast to closely-knit village life, the city is a conglomerate of people from diverse backgrounds and values. Personal ties are diluted by the faster pace of life. Joined by more migrants, urban-dwellers gradually grow into the common mode of not knowing their neighbors, not just the people living next door but also their colleagues. The city nurtures prosperity but also a famine of meaningful relationships.

Cities tend to create a climate of values that define its residents and what their lives are about. As Jacque Ellul writes in *The Meaning of the City*, since Adam's first son Cain, human beings have an innate tendency for city-building as a form of rebellion.[12] The Tower of Babel also arose from the deadly sin of human pride. The free flow of capital, which tends to commodify everything has created a religion in which the worth of individual human beings is measured by their economic productivity, income and possessions. Today's marketplace is also dominated by liturgies of global capitalism and rituals of fetishism. Daniel Groody terms it as "market fundamentalism" or "money-theism."[13] If C. S. Lewis' critiqued the education system's evil in fashioning "men without chests," then the economic system has also successfully abolished the God-ordained dignity of humanity.

In China, most reasons for migration are economically motivated. Migrants move to cities because they are searching for jobs that provide them with food and shelter. Relocation often brings social disorientation, because human beings are limited by sensory contacts with the immediate environment, and thus are prone to lose a sense of familiarity and selfhood when transplanted to a new place. One is forced to emotionally cope with the discontinuities and disempowerment brought by dislocation. The day-to-day problems of local residents may become disproportionate crises for migrants. Feelings of exclusion, estrangement and alienation

12. Ellul, *Meaning of the City*, 1.
13. Groody, *Globalization, Spirituality, and Justice*, 22.

are experienced but are often inexpressible. By voicing "homesickness," a migrant worker is dealing with a whole package of emotions and despair. Very few of them are aware that their difficult circumstances are directly or indirectly caused by unjust regional and global economic policies. They are equally less aware that their self-identities are being reshaped by new forms of oppression in urban industries and latent norms of consumerism. But one thing of which they are acutely conscious is the reality of being caught between two worlds, neither of which is home.

Urban policy-makers look at the influx of migrants from a completely different perspective; they tend to be numbed by statistics. They fail to recognize the human faces of migrants and their disorienting experiences behind these data points. Moreover, their economic localism tends to portray migrant workers as a threat in job competition. Whenever an economic downturn hits, business owners and urban administrators conveniently dispose of rural migrants first. As David H. Jensen says, few assumptions "have achieved such gospel status in public discourse and working practice" like the conception of scarcity.[14] Theologically speaking, should we accept scarcity as given? As Christians, we acknowledge that the world belongs to a God who lavishes abundant material and spiritual blessings on its creatures. Scarcity did not exist in the beginning; it is not supposed to be here. Part of it was a consequence of the Fall (Gen 3:17–19), but another larger part of it, according to William T. Cavanaugh is due to the "pathologies of desires."[15] And in today's world, even our desires have been globalized. Young people shopping in New York and in Shanghai all line up early at Apple stores for the latest product release. To the Chinese, globalization may seem to offer more free choices in the world market, but as consumers, they are being shaped into the same powerless nodes of a vast capitalist domination. While rural migrants enjoy the freedom to be voluntary consumers, just like their urban counterparts, they are actually in turn "being consumed" by a system of manipulative marketing firms and will-

---

14. Jensen, *Responsive Labor*, 6.
15. Cavanaugh, *Being Consumed*, 3.

ful corporations. Urban consumerism presents another source of alienation for rural migrants.

Why are people susceptible to consumerism, including the poor? Cavanaugh insightfully spells it out from a micro-level of social interactions. Primarily, the consumer culture has an inborn tendency to commodify anything. This creates an "inordinate attachment to money and things."[16] Secondly, the shopping culture shapes the human relationship with products as transient and fleeting, "characterized by a constant dissatisfaction with what one already has."[17] Even loyalty programs are commodified and follow the same rule. This builds into the human mentality a cycle of excitement for new things, a fatigue for having them, and then a new excitement for hunting new things. By such constant coveting, the human mind becomes restless, materialistic and unreflective. Cavanaugh is right in concluding that consumerism has a "spiritual disposition" of looking at the world around us, and it is "deeply formative."

The contagious "spend more" consumer culture has powerfully shaped migrants themselves too. Research done by Chinese academics now studies the consumption behaviors of migrant workers.[18] They present two major findings: patterns of conspicuous consumption and the potential for boosting more consumption capacity. Migrants supplement their lack of self-esteem or sense of belonging by purchasing trendy products that symbolize urbanity. Thus, a type of "possessive individualism" forms to compensate for the loss of social status.[19] Policy-makers and businesses are even more covetous in persuading them to spend more by way of commodifying the city community as the ideal. In this way, an rural migrant's attention is diverted from equal citizenship to equality of lifestyle.

---

16. Cavanaugh, *Being Consumed*, 34.

17. Cavanaugh, *Being Consumed*, 34.

18. Huang and Deng, "Rural-to-Urban"; Chu and Zhang, "Chinese Migrants' Consumption."

19. Sheldrake, *Spiritual City*, 140.

Urban consumerism also affects migrant labor at a more macro level. Firstly, when global capital is moving freely across borders, in most cases, labor still cannot. This creates a power imbalance between corporations and workers. Transnational corporations can shop around the globe for the cheapest labor, but local workers in underdeveloped regions have no choice but to accept such employment opportunities. For a long time, China has been the world factory, and the government has used its cheap labor, where workers' wages are frozen for years with a poorly-regulated legal protection environment for national economic advantage. A communist Chinese government coupled with global capital have made a "perfect exploitation." This situation is the context of the Foxconn suicide scenario I mentioned at the beginning of this book.

It is no surprise that authoritarian regimes such as China and Singapore can develop booming market economies. They rely on a well-disciplined labor force to both produce and consume. They overlook the casualties of such practices—the social costs of suicides, deaths from overwork, family disintegration, and the loss of human dignity. Globalization also creates a chain of impersonal relationships that mute the miserable stories behind them. Individual consumers have no idea of the human costs behind their products and services. Globalization has actually dissipated the key dimension of ethical human responsibility for each other in economic transactions. Ironically, globalization creates a sense of transcendent identity, or a "secularized catholicity," as termed by Cavanaugh.[20] It is in this sense that Cavanaugh declares that "consumerism is the death of Christian eschatology" because "there can be no rupture with the status quo, no inbreaking of kingdom of God, but only endless superficial novelty."[21] Urban poverty is to a large extent the result of variant structural absurdities. Here it further convinces us that sin is not just an individual reality; it has taken on an eschatological state of corporate reality.

20. Cavanaugh, *Being Consumed*, 68.
21. Cavanaugh, *Being Consumed*, 93.

Lastly, how then should we view work, the most dominant aspect of urban life? Work makes up a large part of rural migrants' life in the cities. They sacrifice greatly to obtain economic security, often at the cost of not having the whole family together in one place. Poverty and exclusion hit migrant families the hardest because their chances of being both employed and able to responsibly care for children are constrained. However, both the first and second generation struggle to finding work in the cities. To rural migrants, work provides more than just economic security; work affirms dignity. It even provides a sense of pride or gratification to the person. The best test of what makes good work is whether it builds up human relationships.

Work as a whole sets goals to the basic structures of life, such as family and community. The ability to work is a divine gift, beginning in pre-fall Eden. It helps to constitute human personhood. It also shapes our daily behavior, social interactions, and rhythms of life. Sociologist William Julius Wilson claims in his classic work *When Work Disappears* that work imposes healthy disciplines and regularities.[22] This makes work a fundamental aspect of human existence that God has built into the fabric of human nature. As Ben Witherington says, "Work is what weaves together the very fabric of a called person's identity, and fulfills it."[23]

We work because God works. The image of God inside human beings is due to a wellspring of creativity that finds materialization through work. Further, work sustains the natural order that God puts into place. Consequently, the right to meaningful work asserts that joy, freedom, and playfulness be a fundamental part of work's nature and meaning.[24] A person's conception of work always stands in close relationship to his or her understanding of deity or of the meaning of his or her life.[25] Moltmann gives an insightful summary of the meaningfulness of work:

---

22. Wilson, *When Work Disappears*, 73.
23. Witherington, *Work*, 13.
24. Moltmann, *On Human Dignity*, 41.
25. Moltmann, *On Human Dignity*, 40.

> Work is thus meaningful not because it alone provides the meaning of life, but precisely because it is limited by the goal of rest and joy in existence. . . . When people through their work earn their livelihood and produce their life, when they glorify God and partake of his rest on the Sabbath, then they also present themselves before God. Consequently, life has not only a producing value in work, but also a presenting value in the joy of existence. Producing and presenting overflow into each other, for in each production we also present ourselves as we are and as we understand ourselves. Theologically this means that people work and rest "in the presence of God."[26]

Indeed, as Jensen says in *Responsive Labor*, "one of the pathologies of time-crunched individuals is the desire to control time."[27] Obsession with time-efficiency has become a key dimension of urban living. The Christian liturgy of Sabbath rest reinstates an awareness that time is not for our manipulation. It offers a buffer in our consciousness against the totalizing impact of work on people. We are reminded that work should not define too much of who we are. As Miroslav Wolf says, "Work has come to pervade and rule the lives of men and women, be it in the form of indefatigable or cruelly enforced industriousness. . . . Human beings see themselves primarily as "working beings whose highest destiny is to work and whose very being consists in the process of becoming something through work which they would not have been without it."[28] He continues to explain that in today's working culture with its risks of unemployment, being without work seems to put people "outside their life-sustaining environment."[29] But the realization of work and time as God's gifts liberate people, because a society bent on working for achieving things does not expect gifts or grace. The theology of divine gifts in daily working life helps to re-orient us toward gratitude. This becomes even more important in an overworked urban society.

26. Moltmann, *On Human Dignity*, 41.
27. Jensen, *Responsive Labor*, 76.
28. Volf, *Work in the Spirit*, 3.
29. Volf, *Work in the Spirit*, 4.

The attitude toward work in societies unfamiliar with Christian norms followed a different path than the secularization of the Christian roots in Western societies. In societies with a previous influence of Christianity, work went through an uncoupling process of detaching itself not only from any theological sense of purpose, but also from the predominant form of agrarian labor, or in Ben Witherington's term, "the uncoupling of earthling from the earth." In China, however, the change from agricultural work to industrial work has taken a turn more akin to social Darwinism. People's worth or merits are now primarily evaluated based on how their work is remunerated. When a human being must confirm his or her worth through how much he or she earns, as Darrel Cosden says, "human life with its activity ceases to be 'gift.'"[30] In the process of working to achieve one's worth, people find themselves in a frantic, alienated form of existence that prevails in today's global economy.

---

30. Cosden, *Theology of Work*, 11.

4

The Loss of Community

> We have all known the long loneliness, and we
> have found that the answer is community.
>
> —Dorothy Day

> When community is lost, a part of humanity is lost too.
>
> —Anonymous

RURAL MIGRANTS IN CHINA, like immigrants elsewhere, cherish a "land-of-milk-and-honey" illusion prior to migration. Many of them have had urban relatives visiting their countryside hometowns every summer during school breaks, telling them how different and great city life is. Early adventurers brought back samples of modern electronics, and other symbols of urban comfort. TV programs are filled with well-dressed people speaking standardized Mandarin and typing in front of computers as they work in shiny high-rise building or shopping malls, settings in stark contrast with the slow and drab lifestyle in the countryside. Once in the city, however, reality presents the chasm between the earlier fantasy and the later arduousness of daily survival, and between smiley faces on TV programs and the impenetrable apathy from people around them. Furthermore, the migration experience also entails the loss of social connections to one's past. These losses expose individuals to vulnerable situations of greater uncertainty about established rules or implicit "codes of the street," making self-protection a primary concern in social actions. So, the rebuilding of social familiarity toward one's surroundings and the less tangible social norms requires formidable confidence and patience.

In this chapter, I examine the concrete experiences of social integration among rural migrants within their urban neighborhoods. I attempt to get as close as possible to their everyday experiences by drawing on accounts or interpretations of what people actually lived, such as the history and dynamics of their communities, their interactions and identity politics with local residents and authorities, and their efforts in organizing self-help efforts. Drawing on such empirical evidence, I explore the social and political context behind their urban socialization.

Rural Migrants in Shanghai

A city of immigrants throughout its modern history, Shanghai has been associated with regional prejudice against *waidiren* (foreignlanders). The economy's access to the outside world has not ended the closed nature of its socioeconomic system. In its economy, the city always creates two categories of jobs for Shanghai natives and *waidiren* (people from other places). The non-native poor, living in shanty neighborhoods and taking up menial jobs, has locked them into structuralized poverty. When placed next to urban Shanghainese, rural migrants are subject to the double inferiority of being "non-urban" and also "non-Shanghainese."

Treating local origins as "ethnic" identities in sociological analysis is rarely adopted, partly due to the overwhelmingly majority of the Han people in the population. Since mass migration, ample images in newspapers or TV news present rural migrants as "others," with different looks, attire, habits, and dialects. The public discourse has been creating a stereotypical rural migrant who is assumed to walk outside of the law. However, intergroup prejudice may go both ways. While rural migrants feel excluded from mainstream life in Shanghai, they also tend to cast the average Shanghai native as one who lacks interest in "connecting personally."

Depending on their occupation and social experiences with Shanghai natives, rural migrants living in Pond have a variety of experiences with Shanghai natives. For first-generation rural migrants who came from relatively humble backgrounds, the city offers many "work" opportunities to make them firmly believe that a good work ethic of diligence and honesty will surely be rewarding. As the maxim goes, "As long as you work hard, there's money, and that is something good about city life."

Younger generation migrants with a different reference group than their parents; migrant workers who work in more competitive yet segregated workplaces; or migrants who happen to have been exposed to more prejudices against their place of origin are more prone to react with similar prejudices. Many younger migrants expressed more indignant feelings toward "unequal pay for equal work" and other managerial inequalities for Shanghai natives at their workplaces. Trivial social encounters that randomly happen to rural migrants may heighten or ease such intergroup prejudices. Most rural migrants have a limited chance to interact with Shanghai natives, so the social-psychological effects of these positive or negative incidents are usually critical.

The distinctive Shanghai dialect serves another impenetrable barrier for a *waidiren* to assimilate into daily understandings in the city. It takes a long time for a *waidiren* to acquire this dialect (a formidable task to a *waidiren* myself during my one year of fieldwork in Shanghai). This skill gradually builds up its value of cultural capital until the choice of language becomes a symbol of local familiarity and, thus, superiority. This language of exclusion can be easily translated into a "language of power." For example, Shanghai natives prefer to use their local dialect to get a good bargain, because both parties feel at ease and share emotional closeness while using it. An awareness of "otherness" brings about certain awkwardness to the bewildered *waidiren* in a conversation like this, reinforcing the boundaries of social categorization. A non-native who diligently learns the language but fails to grasp its nuances remains marked as an "other."

THE LOSS OF COMMUNITY

An interesting change took place in 2008 when the government started to promote naming new migrants to the city, a large proportion of whom were rural migrants, as "New Shanghainese" (*xin* Shanghai-*ren*). It was an attempt to alleviate the discriminatory label of "*nongmingong*" (peasant-workers). This re-naming had little effect in improving the status of rural migrants than changing "temporary permit" into "resident permit." Rural migrants' identity as a distinctive status group is constructed through enduring status-laden socioeconomic processes.

The expansion of urban space took place after the disintegration of the urban *danwei* system. Compared to western cities where residents could self-govern, cities in socialist China were turned into sites of industrial production that were austerely divided into small grids of the *danwei* system. Only one organizational infrastructure is left—the "street committees" (*juweihui*), which are vigilant coordinators in the system of social control and the basic organizational form of party influence in cities. By 1990, China had 5099 such units in 447 cities, each staffed by a dozen full-time employees and half-time retirees.[1] These street committees function in enforcing family-planning policies, hygiene inspection, mediating conflicts, etc. Since the 1990s, as state budgets for street committees dropped, they were left to generate additional funds on their own through various self-initiated economic activities. This background information will be useful in later analysis.

Shanghai has a long history of spatial segregation. Patches of low-rise "*penghuqu*" (shanty neighborhoods) inhabited by immigrants and the urban poor were spawned along two sides of the Suzhou River as well as behind the back alleys in the commercial districts. These "poverty belts" surrounded Shanghai's foreign concessions and urban communities since the 1940s. In 1949, there were still 1109 square meters of "*penghuqu*" in the city accommodating a migrant population of around 1.15 million.[2] Space and poverty reinforced each other here, producing a type of chronic poverty for *penghu qu* residents. They comprised the bulk

1. Zhan and Li, *Grassroots Governance*, 15.
2. Chen, *Life and Memory*.

of Shanghai's urban poor, with a unique lifestyle that formed an invisible wall against urban integration. Since the 1980s, Shanghai's *penghu* areas became destinations for rural migrants from Shanghai's neighboring provinces, at first solo migrants followed by long-term-stay families.

Some existing *penghu* areas became dominated by migrants, with only a handful of senior locals who are reluctant to move, breeding a unique mixing of locals and migrants. *Subei* (from Northern Jiangsu province) people in these areas generally live on good terms with their tenants, who came primarily from Anhui, and Jiangxi. In the community where I conducted participant observation, some *subei* Shanghainese offered generous help in referring us to people they knew. They tend to form some sentimental connection with rural migrant families, because the latter live in a way that is reminiscent of what life was like for Subei migrants several decades before. At different historical junctures, both groups suffered from institutionalized inferiority and were pushed to the margins of the urban economy.

Pond: An Urban Slum in Central Shanghai

Behind the façades of Shanghai's glamorous Millennium Shopping Center, a crowded area of one-story shanty buildings, lies in sharp contrast to its high-rise skyscraper surroundings. A completely different world is concealed there, separated by just one street. I name this rural migrant community "The Pond," because its Chinese name contains the character *tang*, which means "pond." The name suits the self-contained lifestyle of this neighborhood, possessing a different ecology than the rest of Shanghai.

The Pond is not an area one could locate on the map, but with over two thousand households packed into this small patch of land, it is not easy to miss either. It is located at the crossroads of Pond Street, a major road that cuts through a few districts, and the more narrow and unimpressive Northrain Street in M district. This area is well known as an "industrial zone" set up by the district government since the 1990s. Pond is surrounded by a few factories that manufacture food and electronics.

The entrance to the Pond is a small gate in the wall that allows only pedestrians to enter. Inside the Pond, one will soon detect a web of half-hidden lanes intersecting with each other and dividing the area into ten blocks. The total number of inhabitants, estimated by Zeng, the director of the Pond street committee, has exceeded one third of the total migrant population in M district.

In collaboration with the research team of the local NGO ROOT (which I also served as a regular volunteer to teach children English), I conducted a household survey (N = 52) in November of 2007. The fifty-two households were selected from ten administrative teams ("blocks") as classified by the street committee. Questions concerning basic demographic information (i.e. gender, education, *hukou* origin, jobs, income), family make-up, duration of stay in the city, number of children, parental involvement with children, presence of relatives in the neighborhood, etc. The purpose was to gain a broader picture of the neighborhood composition and family sizes. It was also critical to gain the trust of many families through this formal presentation supported by the street committee. I had the opportunity to go back and do in-depth interviews with over a dozen families who had responded to this survey.

The survey certainly had several constraints. First was the sampling method. Because the questionnaires were administered only during weekends, the sampling failed to include many rural migrants who were at work during that time. Since we only interviewed whoever was at home during the weekend for each household, the unemployment rate is likely to be over-reported (11 percent). Likewise, the percentage of female respondents (60 percent) is uncharacteristically high. Secondly, due to time constraints, I excluded some variables about their work and neighborhood effects. With these limitations, however, the dataset still serves its purpose in setting the broader demographic framework of this group of rural migrants I studied.

I learned from the street committee and education officials that in Shanghai, over sixty percent of the rural migrants come from rural Anhui; they also tend to be limited to a few informal lines of work: recycling, street vending, and interior renovation. The presence of entrepreneurial Fujian rural migrants made the Pond distinct from other neighborhoods that are predominantly inhabited by Anhui migrants. In terms of how long they have lived in the city of Shanghai, 15.7 percent answered "more than ten years," and 54.9 percent "six to ten years." Less than ten percent of respondents belong to the subset of short-term seasonal migrants. This trend of long-term settlement of rural migrants in the city, a recent development since the late 1990s, is confirmed in the Pond.

When asked about the size of their nuclear families, over half of the respondents reported having more than two children, and even 11.5 percent had three children. Compared to the average Shanghai urban family with one child, rural migrant families presented the city with a baby boom. Survey results also show that 87.8 percent of families with children brought their firstborns to attend schools in Shanghai. From casual conversations, I notice that families with more than two children generally face economic difficulties due to both educational investment and the huge economic penalties for violating the one-child policy. In some areas of rural Anhui, such a violation may amount to 100 thousand *yuan* (one-time), roughly two to three years of household income for that family.

Over fifty percent of rural migrants in the Pond received education equal to or less than junior middle school. The gap in income levels between rural migrants at the Pond and other Shanghai residents is seen from an indirect comparison. Since we asked respondents for the *range* of their monthly household incomes, it is hard to compute an average figure that can be compared to the annual per capita income of an average Shanghai resident, which reached 26,675 yuan in 2008. Based on this, an average Shanghai family of three individuals make a monthly income of around 7000 to 8000 yuan. The majority of rural migrants (63.5 percent) with an average family size of three to four individuals in a household make less than 3500 yuan per month. Only 3.8 percent of Pond families made more than 5001 yuan a month. This small proportion of relatively well-to-do rural migrant families may number about 200 households in the Pond.

Just a wall apart from the shopping center, the Pond surprises every newcomer by its sudden compression of space and the striking dynamism of its market activities. When walking into its ten-foot-wide "main street," a newcomer may be busy to avoid bumping into the eye-catching signs on both sides. The neighborhood bustles with activity from dawn to dusk, with two major "market streets" attracting a constant flow of people. There are constantly traders passing by on bicycles or tricycles carrying loads of vegetables, bottled water, or other goods for delivery, and there are customers waiting at food stands for their meals, women chatting with house chores in their hands, unattended schoolchildren playing in narrow and muddy alleys, and a few jobless adolescents strolling around to pass time.

The small lanes are filled with a mixture of smells from restaurants, barber shops, snack stores, pancake stands, seafood stands, and public restrooms. There are over 200 shops, grocery stores and small diners at the Pond. They cover almost every need and necessity. Some signs indicate regional food, such as Shandong Dumplings, Sichuan Stir fries, and Henan Noodles. All shops here belong to the grey sector of "unlicensed" businesses. Shops are flung open for the curious eyes of an occasional visitor. Here, the limited space does not allow the luxury of personal "privacy." So, one may notice that these business people live inside their shops. On top of each shop space, there is a box-shaped bed hanging down the ceiling for the shop owners to sleep in at night. During the daytime, they climb down and lay out their items or dishes. At night, the shop is turned into the living room and bedroom. Private bath facilities are impossible to find. People use a public bathhouse nearby, which sells tickets for eight yuan per person.

My fieldwork observations in Shanghai, Beijing and Wuhan show that concentration by *hukou* origin and occupational clustering are noticeable characteristics of rural migrant communities.

Some villages in suburban Beijing are literally the "spatial transplantation" of some rural Hebei or Henan villages. One can detect few traces of urban integration except that each family mounts a picture taken at the Tian'anmen Square, an indication of their current location and a sense of national pride of living in the capital city. In Shanghai, rural migrants populate both inner city and suburban areas, but recent years have seen a trend of suburbanization among this population. In inner city neighborhoods, sometimes two or three families share a roof. Rooms for rent come in all sizes, because local landlords separate old housing units into compartments of all sizes. Some are terribly small that only one person can sleep in. I once saw a newcomer bargaining with a local landlord over a "room" that looked like a cell with one bed but no window. The landlord lady insisted on 300 yuan a month.[3] The new arrival just frowned and stood in silent negotiation. I took a deep breath while imagining myself sleeping with eyes wide open in this box-like cement cell.

A typical migrant family often uses a bunk bed, with children sleeping on the top, and parents on lower level. A used TV set is a must-have amenity in every family. Cupboards outside of the living space are for cooking. Due to the centrality of Pond community, rent is much higher than other places. "For Rent" signs are seldom seen, however. In this "popular" area, information is quickly circulated through well-connected landlords.

Over twenty percent of migrants living in the Pond came from Fujian province. They belong to a very entrepreneurial group. The process for them to enter the business market in the Pond was very similar to Beijing's "Zhejiang village" around that time. In the beginning, with increasing flows of rural migrants, grassroots administrators (street committees) considered informal businesses

---

3. For this amount, one can rent a room that is three times larger in suburban Shanghai. According to the China Household Income Project (CHIP) survey results in 2002, over 55 percent of rural migrant workers had a living area of less than ten square meters. Housing costs are a big financial burden for them due to rising rents and stagnation in wage growth. According to the CHIP survey, rent accounted for almost half of rural migrants' total household expenditure.

THE LOSS OF COMMUNITY

a good way to "create job opportunities" and to avoid instability. They even collaborated with rural migrants in maintaining market order. For a time, the Pond market was so prosperous that it attracted substantial media attention. But the prosperity of the Pond market did not last long. Chaotic land ownership issues and the short-term orientation of market building by Fujian migrants eventually resulted in deteriorating infrastructure. In 2002, authorities listed "overcrowding" and the "failure to pass inspection of fire preventative infrastructure" as reasons for demolition. "Our top officials were just afraid that it would become too '*luan*' (chaotic) here," recalled a staff at the street committee.

After 2003, the composition of Pond residents changed dramatically, from the more entrepreneurial Fujian migrants to a much poorer group of Anhui migrants.[4] Poverty migration characterizes rural migrants from Anhui. These new tenants of the Pond used to inhabit a slum area near a deserted railway intersection. The image of inflowing "vagrants" terrified the local administrators at Pond. Together with the local Public Security Bureau, they spent a week checking migrants' permits. Similar surveillance was carried out on a weekly basis afterwards.

Some background information here is necessary. Detention and deportation were part of the collective memory of rural migrants in China's big cities from 1996 to 2003. Regulations to control rural migrants brought a lucrative business to police stations, as rural migrants became frequent targets of forced bribery, repatriation and physical violence. For each detainee, fines and bribes could add up to several hundred yuan. In Shanghai, 40,000

---

4. Anhui is known as one of China's largest agricultural provinces, sometimes a euphemism for a disadvantaged area. In history, poverty of the peasants was also especially acute because of the flooding of the Huai River. The most flooding took place around 1991. The region's GDP per capita only amounts to one third of the level of its two neighboring provinces, Zhejiang and Jiangsu. According to a survey conducted by the Anhui government, on average one out of six Anhui residents out-migrated in 2004, and the number kept increasing each year. Around 24.5 percent of these out-migrating peasants come to Shanghai. In 2003, over 570 thousand children from age five to fourteen followed their parents to other cities, consisting of up to 6 percent of the total out-migrating population from Anhui.

detentions and deportations were reported in 1993; the number doubled in 1996, then rose to 100,000 in 1997.[5]

According to staff of the Pond Street Committee, the rural migrants from Anhui were a totally different group. If the demolition of the Pond market once left them with lingering frustration, they felt equally reluctant to welcome such a change. It is clear that from the beginning, the Pond Street Committee has associated "criminality" with the new rural migrants, and it has adopted a suspicious and exclusive attitude toward them. A social fabric of mutual trust and reciprocity was absent from the onset of their relationship. Here, high mobility and turnover continue to create a prevalent anonymity that breaks communal identity into pieces. The Pond became a laboratory of social despair.

Since 2005, urban street committees underwent a reform, which left them on their own initiative to "generate revenues" to cover staff wages. They came up with the idea of market reconstruction. Wei, the director of the Pond street committee, went to the Bureau of Commerce and Business inquiring about the possibility of allowing informal businesses for rural migrants in their administrative community. Wei recalls, "they allowed us to charge management fees and organize the market here. Their only concern was about food security. Thus, we required people who opened restaurants and diners here to have health permits." From talking with Wei, I sense that it was much to the local street committee's advantage to allow informal businesses here, because their staff's salaries depend mainly on collecting management fees from its over 200 rental spaces. The relationship between local administrators and rural migrants in the Pond has been characterized by an odd mixture of dependency and domination.

Categorization is an ongoing process for the Pond's local governance. Since June of 2002, Shanghai changed its "temporary residence permit" system into a new "residence permit" system with three main categories: "skilled/talent" (*rencai lei*), "work" (*congye lei*), and "dependent" (*toukao lei*). Despite superficial differences, it is a mere name-change when it comes to implementation. As

---

5. Unger, *Transformation of Rural China*, 35; Shukai, "Criminality," 102.

French sociologist Bourdieu claims, the process of social categorization, of "making things explicit and classifying them," is a key mechanism of "identity-making of social control."[6] The act of "registration" symbolizes a certain power relationship among social status groups. Public administrators can freely levy fees or release governance measures that entail different attitudes toward members and non-members of this system, and such practices forcefully reproduce the distinct social identity of the rural class. Though such social control devices are considered as indispensable by local administrators, many rural migrants see them as of "no use" and a "hassle." As a way of defying authority, they simply would not show up at registration windows. They also became aloof toward the one-child policy, which used to be the toughest social control mechanism.

Experiences of Migrant Families

Given the predominant presence of migrant families with children at Pond (over two thirds), routines and accidents related to children make up the story lines at the Pond. Education is also a non-threatening topic that most rural migrants like to talk about, which often dispels the distrust and brings those conversing in closer touch with life's concerns. I selected four families to present in more detail how their life chances were limited by the interlocking effects of informal employment, negative neighborhood effects, and inherited inequality across generations.

The Zhangs

The Zhangs live in a room of around fifteen square meters with their three children. A double bunk bed takes up half of the space. Zhang's older daughter Jing sleeps on the top bunk, side by side with her younger brother. The couple and their youngest son sleep at the bottom level. Beside the bed, there is a lower writing table

---

6. Bourdieu, *Language and Symbolic Power*.

loaded with used books and paper boxes. In the summer when it gets too hot and humid in the room, the boys would make this writing table into their bed. Like other families here, they set up an extended area outside the window for cooking using a recycled cupboard. All the furniture in the room is pushed against the walls in order to make more space. The television and other small electronics in the dwelling were items that the Zhangs found on their daily recycling routes.

Mr. Zhang is a heavily built northern man. The heavy penalty for having three children left them in debt, the main reason they left for the city. The couple first worked at a few construction sites, leaving the children with grandparents. Then after a few years, their economic condition improved, so they decided to bring the children with them.

"I never went to school," says Zhang's wife, "but after all, a good education for the children is most important." So, the whole family moved to the Pond in 2000, because Zhang's relatives already lived here. They chose to do recycling because this job allows them to freely allocate time to care for the three children.

At that time, there was a migrant school inside the Pond community, with over 900 migrant children enrolled. It offered courses from grade one to the second year of junior middle (equivalent to grade seven). Afterwards, most students will need to return to their *hukou* origin for the final year of junior middle, which will prepare them for the entrance exam to senior middle school. Although they were unhappy with the quality of teaching in this migrant school, the Zhangs enrolled their three children in this school since no other schools in the proximity received migrant children.

Just like the fate of the Pond market, the Pond migrant school launched into operation with some informal head-nods from the street committee. Its closedown was foretold by its illegitimacy. In 2003, the M district government decided that there should not be any migrant schools inside its administrative region. This was another turbulent event for the Pond people. Eligible transfers into public schools needed to go through the district Education Bureau, with several required documents, such as proof of employment and vaccination, from the parents.

Since most families in the Pond took up informal jobs such as domestic cleaning, delivery, recycling, and street vending, many do not possess any type of work permit. Only a few managed to get proofs of work status through personal connections. No statistics were available to see how many children were not transferred smoothly that year. But according to the Pond street committee staff, only four hundred migrant families came for vaccination certificates.

The two months after the school's shut down were most difficult for the Zhang family. As recyclers, Zhang never possessed any "work permit" to prove his working status. The couple asked around anxiously, and they used all their connections to get a fake paper for Zhang as a temporary worker at some factory. Then Zhang's wife lined up in front of the education bureau office for a whole month, hoping to get three registration forms for her children. When it was announced that the quota had been filled, she turned in distress and found her motorcycle stolen. Mrs. Zhang broke down. Her condition was noticed by an official in the education bureau. Out of sympathy, that official secured three quotas for her. Since the re-allocation of students was completely arbitrary and slots were randomly drawn, Zhang's three children attend three different public primary schools in that area. Although Zhang now needs to spend more time taking each to school by motorcycle, he is very content. Since 2007, tuition fees for primary school pupils were waived, so the children are enjoying a much better learning environment with much lower costs. The two boys, eleven-year-old Ming and eight-year-old Jun have developed an interest in playing some musical instruments at school, so the parents are on the lookout for old instrument parts during their recycling work.

Boy Jet and the Liangs

Not all the Pond families went through such a smooth adjustment after the school closure. Jet's story is another case. The boy was said to be such a slow learner at the public school that his teachers hesitated to allow him to move on to third grade. Jet's mother is illiterate herself, and the father has been too busy to care for his homework, so Jet's grades continued to drop.

One Saturday morning, I met ten-year-old Jet for the first time in an English class when I was volunteering for ROOT, an NGO in Pond community. Since then, Jet became my "tour guide" for the webs of small alleys inside the Pond, and he seemed to enjoy it. Familiar with every small hidden turn, here and there, he is proud of his "local knowledge" that I had not acquired. Jet and his parents moved to this area seven years ago, when he was only a toddler. The mud and chaos that puts off an intruder from the outside like myself has always been his familiar playground.

Jet is not a clean boy. A closer look at him show that his parents were raising the boy carelessly: his hair has grown into long strands, without being washed probably for a long time; his sky blue school uniform is turning grey and is marked with dots of mud and ink. Most strikingly, as he stretches out his forearms, long bruises and scars jumped into my eyes. "My dad beat me up again," he explains to me.

"Why did he do that?" I asked, while suppressing my angry surprise. Then Jet bowed down his head and murmured, "because I went to play video games again . . . " I knew the boy was not doing well in his schoolwork, but I was not informed of the domestic violence happening in his family. So, I decided to visit Jet's parents the next day.

Jet's father, Liang, forty, had opened a snack shop in the Pond, selling soft drinks, snacks, and bubble tea. It's a tiny space of only four to five square meters. From seven to ten in the morning, Liang's shop also sells fried pancakes (*jianbing*), a type of northern regional breakfast. I visited him when he was working at the pancake stand. I asked how many he usually sells per day. "Usually over a hundred," he said, "two yuan each." When business subsided after 10 a.m., he sat down and talked to me. He continued the conversation by telling about rising living costs. Now he pays 450 yuan for this teashop, a rent double that of last year. Another 300 yuan goes for the living room they rent at the back, where the family spends the nights. The teashop is too small to hold a bed, as in other rental spaces.

Liang appeared to have a mild temperament when talking to me. I almost hesitated to associate this mild-tempered father with the scars on Jet's forearms. Trying to change the subject from business to his son, I asked, "You know Jet came to my English class on Saturday? He did well, just a little bit distracted from time to time. Do you find it difficult to discipline him?"

Liang seemed to know that I was referring to, and he replied, "The boy is too hard to discipline, always spending money and time in video game rooms . . . Sometimes we could not find him anywhere, and we get anxious. Then every time I would find him playing a video game again! He simply wouldn't listen. So, I spanked him hard." Pausing for a few seconds, Liang continued, "I know I shouldn't beat him . . . You see, we had my son when I was in my late thirties. People say it is a blessing for an older man to have his first son. I did not want to treat him like that, but it's the only way that works for him!"

Liang had a long, tough journey to the city. He left northern Jiangsu (*subei*) at the age of twenty after his mother passed away. With no close relatives to rely on, Liang came to Shanghai. He did all kinds of work, such as construction, renovation, factory work, etc. He sometimes liked drinking and hanging out with friends, so he never had much savings, which made it difficult for him to date any women. Liang later met his wife, who is ten years younger than he. "Because she also came from a poor family and did not go to school, she did not look down upon me," Liang told me with a shy smile. So, the couple had their son when Liang was thirty-eight years old. Since then, they picked up street vending, because it allows more freedom to care for the child. They both value education very much.

Jet's first grade was also spent in the migrant school at the Pond. After its demolition, the boy was admitted to a public school, under the condition that the boy should re-take Grade One courses. Like the Zhang family, Liang also had to stop the business, and return to his place of *hukou* origin for necessary paperwork, which cost him several thousand yuan. When Jet continued to Grade Two, his school performance started to drop. Both Jet's parents and the teachers knew the direct cause to be the boy's addiction to video games.

Migrant-concentrated neighborhoods do not offer a positive learning environment for migrants' second generation. With overcrowding and lack of spaces, the community offers exposure to many undesirable resources, such as video game rooms, "internet bars" and small gambling casinos. These amenities flourish in the hidden lanes of the Pond. Some businesses are located inside some family dwellings. With no external signs or advertisements, they are verbally broadcasted among dropout kids and jobless adults. Insufficient parental involvement in their coursework is actually the deeper root cause for children's engagement with these activities.

According to the community survey, parents are generally less educated (with 9.6 percent illiteracy, and the most educated 48 percent having just a junior middle school education). Burdened with the daily pressure to make more money, most parents seldom spend time in helping with their children's homework. Most children in the Pond wear keys around their necks. Some commute to schools by themselves, and come home to cook for themselves. Their parents work in nearby factories, often arriving home after 10 p.m. These "latch-key kids" are susceptible to addiction to video games. The Pond offers no playground or recreational sites other than narrow street corners for the children here. That problem has created a "market" for video game businesses and internet bars. These places function as the socialization arena for children at the Pond.

Migrant children at play (courtesy of Joann Pittman)

The next time I went to tutor Jet's English, his mother, Wang, shyly asked me if I could do them a favor by accompanying her to Jet's school some day. It turned out that the school had demanded that Jet's parents transfer him immediately. Not wanting her son to experience so much disruption, Wang wanted to talk with the public school for one last time, and she wanted me to go along with her.

Wang usually takes care of the teashop early from 6 a.m. to 4 p.m. in the afternoon, then goes to pick up Jet from school. We went to the school around the usual time. Standing at the door of Jet's classroom, I noticed the boy sitting in the last row, obviously distracted while other students were writing. The math teacher immediately noticed Wang, and frowned with obvious contempt. She angrily reproached her loudly while pointing at Jet, "Your child could not answer any quiz questions today! He even makes noises when others are studying. Look at his quiz yourself!!" Jet's quiz paper was thrown at Wang's face. She picked it up, and her face was all red.

Soon we were brought to see the director of Jet's class, his Chinese teacher Lu. Lu likewise frowned at the sight of Wang, and with impatience in her tone, she said, "I am telling you again, this boy should not stay in class if he does not do any homework and cannot catch up." She remained in her seated position while Wang and I stood in front of her desk, with sorry looks on our faces, like two students who are caught in wrongdoing. All the teachers in the office looked at us, and then Wang apologized for her son's misbehavior, her voice trembling and close to tears.

"And who are you?" Teacher Lu asked, spotting me as a stranger. I introduced myself as a volunteer mentor for Jet in the Pond. With some confusion, she looked at me. Then I explained that we are a group of social workers who are trying to help children like Jet to catch up in coursework. "That's no use," she uttered abruptly. "This boy is hopeless! Just look at him! He does not even wash his hair and his clothes." She then turns to Wang and scolded her. "What type of parents are you? And now you bring a college student to support you? That's no use!!" Wang continued to apologize for a few more seconds, then we were told to leave.

After this trip, ROOT volunteers, including myself, tried harder to help Jet's schoolwork. For about a month, Jet seemed to be learning well, and even stopped going to video games. His father was grateful for our help, and agreed to stop spanking him. Things went peacefully for two months, until one day, after my English class, Jet showed me the new bruises on his arms.

The same month, Jet's school insisted on his immediate transfer, and that Jet should not take part in the final exams. "What do you plan to do?" I asked Liang. He said the only option would be to transfer Jet to the migrant school five miles away from the Pond. Liang also decided to let Jet re-take Grade Two, since the boy did not learn much in the past year. Again? I thought to myself. This would make Jet the oldest student in his class. "A good thing is, I think he will be happy in that [migrant] school. At least the teachers would not look down at them." Liang says to me.

About one third of primary-school-age children at the Pond attend this migrant school, because it's the only migrant school in the adjacent area. The enrolled number once reached a record high of 1300 students. Since adjacent public schools only take in first-born children from families with appropriate documents, most families with two or more children had to send their younger children to this migrant school. Many share experiences similar to Jet, entering and dropping out of public schools.

Boy Qiang and His Father

As poor a community as the Pond is, most families there value children's education. The vast majority of school-age children, even there, are enrolled in school. But when a child is identified as "being on the street" rather than properly schooled, a social stigma is attached to the family.

Eight-year-old Qiang is probably the youngest dropout. His parents moved into the Pond about seven years ago. The family came from Henan province. Qiang's father had a hard time finding jobs, and ended up addicted to gambling with a jobless group at the Pond. This situation soon sent the family into dire poverty. For years, Qiang's mother strove to find irregular jobs to sustain their livelihood. When Qiang reached the age of five, his father refused to give up gambling, so his mother walked out of the home and never came back. This change pulled Qiang's father out of gambling but into deep depression. After he was able to pull himself together and find some work, Qiang had been unschooled for a year.

Many families would sympathetically send the boy some food when his father was drunk or out at work. But most of them would not let their children play with Qiang. The family had only a bed, a TV set, a lamp, and a rice cooker in the single room. When his father goes out for work, Qiang cooks some rice for himself. This explains why the boy always looked pale and undernourished. Qiang's father did find a job, as a night janitor for a hospital nearby. He started to ride his bike to work every evening, and came back the next morning. During the day, Qiang had to find something to do by himself while his father slept at home. The boy was very isolated. He occasionally visited the video game rooms but had no money to play. He was looking forward to a new semester, because his father promised to send him to school again in September. We were all glad about how things were working out for the boy, and he showed more interest in learning in our after-school programs.

However, life is often disturbed by unexpected tragedies. As ROOT volunteers, we always discussed safety concerns for children in this neighborhood. The two intersecting roads surrounding are often busy with traffic. Although everyone sensed the potential risks with children running around in that area, nobody took measures to prevent bad things from happening.

I was not in Shanghai when my friends at ROOT sent me the news report describing an accident in the Pond area, with two unschooled boys run over by a bus. It was confirmed that the two boys were Jet and Qiang. With his arm and leg muscles severely injured, Jet had been in coma for three days, while Qiang was killed instantly.

Jet's accident changed the family's trajectory in the city completely. The couple closed down their teashop so that they could take shifts in caring for Jet, who still needed to undergo a few surgeries. They did keep their living space in the Pond. Everyday Jet's father cooks and brings the meals over to the hospital, where his wife stays overnight. Liang told me that when he heard of the accident, he cried because he thought he was going to lose his son.

Regrets overwhelmed him, as he recollected, and he vowed, "I would never force him to study or beat him. I feel so content that he is alive and well now."

In this tragic incident, the bus driver was at fault by crossing the pedestrian walkway during a red light, so the two families were guaranteed some compensation. The tragedy, lawsuits, and compensation became the number one conversation topic at the Pond. Qiang and his family became the focus. The boy's father was devastated and felt guilty for his negligence. Qiang's mother, who had been gone for over three years, reappeared at Qiang's funeral, also crushed.

Mixed feelings of criticism and sympathy stirred up people's conversations. Every family started to warn their kids from running outdoors. ROOT volunteers held meetings to discuss how to reduce potential dangers in the community, and to help the two families get timely compensation. A communal response emerged, but such a heightened state lasted for about a month before the Pond returned to its old way of life.

The Wans

Many children of migrant families experience dislocation from rural to urban and then from urban to rural again. These continual adjustments are usually ill-handled. Sometimes the disoriented child becomes a crisis point for the whole family, as shown in the Wan family's story.

Wan's family is much admired in the Pond. The couple, at the time of contact, makes about twice the income of an average migrant family. Both parents have quite decent jobs—Wan has been a domestic maid for an expatriate American family for the past two years. Working for foreigners not only adds to the prestige of her job; Wan is also seen as lucky to have met a kindhearted foreigner who soon found a job for her husband as well. Now they are probably economically better off than many local Shanghainese. For the past three years, the family lived contently, with their youngest son slowly discovered his talent in music and art, and two older daughters growing into teenage lifestyles in the city. But a crisis approached after Wan's oldest daughter Ling returned home for middle school.

One out of five families at the Pond is incomplete, not by divorce, but due to family members living apart. Either the couple has left their children home with their grandparents, or one of them left to accompany their post-primary-school-age children for further education back home. Making this decision was not easy. Wan had reasons to worry that such a drastic change would seem almost like "exile" to the young girl, who barely understands the difficulties facing her parents. Wan's husband accompanied their two teenage girls back to rural Anhui. With her worries and pain after their separation, Wan pulled herself together because life has to move on. The couple started to invest even more into the youngest boy. Two years later, the time came when their son was not allowed to move up to middle school. Wan went back to find an elite boarding middle school in the nearest township. "Tuition and living expenses cost a total of 6000 yuan per term," says Wan, "but it's the best middle school in our township."

The three children went through their ups and downs in varying degrees. Wan's worries were confirmed when her oldest daughter suddenly decided to quit school. "She had been into pop music and boys," Wan told me, and started to blame herself for the decision to leave her in the countryside. "My daughter always says to me, 'Don't blame me, mama, if I could not achieve what you expected.' I said I would not, you just try your best, and I would not blame you on whatever turns out . . . We were not able to provide them good opportunities. Now I really regret bringing them to Shanghai at the beginning. It would have been much better if we let them stay in the countryside . . . So it's not their fault."

I heard similar comments from a few families at Pond, "We regret bringing our children along to Shanghai . . . they could have done better in school at home." Actually, most families are unprepared to determine which school their children could attend in Shanghai. Many had rosy expectations about their children's chances of getting into formal schools. But their social networks and information channels are so limited that it is impossible for them to do any research or locate schools. Many parents ended up sending children to the closest migrant schools they could find.

An intense crisis disrupted the couple's work when Ling left home with a simple goodbye note. The direct cause was that the Ling and another teenage boy in her class, because of their romantic involvement, became the targets of blame by parents and teachers. For the next two days, Wan and her husband checked every familiar corner of the nearby streets, parks, and the railway station where Ling could possibly have been. They spent several sleepless nights before Ling finally called back from a Suzhou factory, where she had found a temporary job.

Theological Reflections: Community Breakdown as Human Suffering

The breakdown of community in China's post-socialist context presents a more dramatic change than its counterpart in Western societies. For rural migrants, it equaled the disintegration of a rigid form of militant collectivism lived in rural communes. Following the initial flow of solo migrants, the traditional form of Chinese family also disintegrated. Matching the dominant model of "one family, two locations" for rural migrants, the divorce rate in rural families is also rocketing. Later, when children of rural *hukou* origin joined their parents in Chinese cities, the educational paths of these youngsters followed truncated phases of instability and dislocation such that a sense of community with their teachers, parents and peers was also lost to them. Migrant schools in the city are also characterized by high turnover rates among teachers and students. It seems that all their social relationships are fragmented and transient, just as Zygmunt Bauman poignantly describes:

> Gone is the certainty that "we will meet again," that we will be meeting repeatedly and for a very long time to come—and that therefore society can be presumed to have a long memory and what we do to each other today will come to comfort us or grieve us in the future;

that what we do with each other has more than episodic significance.[7]

Human beings need community because they are made in the image of God, the ultimate diversity in unity. No one can flourish in isolation. His or her selfhood and spiritual needs are to be realized in communal life, including family, workplace, school, neighborhood, and church. The need for community is part of what it means to be a human person; as Aristotle says, "Anyone who either cannot lead the common life or is so self-sufficient as not to need to, and therefore does not partake of society, is either a beast or a god."[8] Jürgen Moltmann concurs when he affirms that "the image of God is human beings together with others. Only in human fellowship with other people is the human person truly the image of God (Gen 1:28)."[9] Attitudes of solidarity in these smaller communities have practical consequences for politics, economics and social action. Thus, each human being is responsible through communal involvement for the wellbeing of the whole society.

What has turned so many rural migrant communities (including its families, workplaces, neighborhoods, schools and even churches) into spaces of despair? The answer lies largely in what I have laid out in the preceding two chapters of this book. But more broadly, the loss of human community has been a crisis of contemporary societies, east and west. In his classic sociological study *Bowling Alone: The Collapse and Revival of American Community*, Robert D. Putnam claims that community bonds in affluent America "have weakened steadily throughout our history," leading to a "civic malaise."[10] It may not be not poverty alone as the main factor that leads to community breakdown; it is almost an eschatological sign. Significantly, Friedrich Nietzsche depicts "the last man" as human beings who are tired of life, take no risks, and seek only comfort and security. As a result, society is

---

7. Bauman, *Community*, 47–48.
8. Aristotle, *Politics* 1.1253a.
9. Moltmann, *On Human Dignity*, 25.
10. Putnam, *Bowling Alone*, 25.

not flourishing but is full of mediocrity and apathy. For the social outcast, it tends to be worse, just as Bauman notes about residents of ghettos: "sharing stigma and public humiliation does not make the sufferers into brothers; it feeds mutual derision, contempt and hatred."[11] This reminds me of an unusual scene inside a poor migrant community in suburban Beijing—a row of over thirty squat toilet units were individually locked, allowing only one family to use each unit. This sight made mutual distrust and fear among migrants themselves very obvious. I was struck by how building a public restroom can become an impossible task for collaboration among the poor. It left me with a deep impression of community breakdown as a form of human suffering.

Community has deep theological significance, as its variant term "communion" embodies. Human beings are born with the need for connection, solidarity, and interdependence. Communal shalom is the extension of internal peace with God to social relationships. It is the opposite of alienation. In this sense, when the first human community broke down, Adam's sin was essentially a withdrawal into self-love. Since then, individualism has given rise to social conflicts that continue to plague human society. Reinhold Niebuhr points out:

> Whatever increase in social intelligence and moral goodwill may be achieved in human history, may serve to mitigate the brutalities of social conflict, but they cannot abolish the conflict itself. That could be accomplished only if human groups, whether racial, national or economic, could achieve a degree of reason and sympathy which would permit them to see and to understand the interests of others as vividly as they understand their own, and a moral goodwill which would prompt them to affirm the rights of others as vigorously as they affirm their own.[12]

At the same time, as Moltmann says, "the community which calls Jesus 'Son of Man' suffers under the ongoing inhumanity

---

11. Bauman, *Community*, 121.
12. Niebuhr, *Moral Man and Immoral Society*, xxiii–xxiv.

and dehumanization of human beings, and through its prayers turns this suffering into a painful awareness."[13] I think any active involvement with community-rebuilding ought to start with this painful awareness.

Historians find that flourishing cities have always had three functions: the provision of security, the hosting of commerce, and the creation of sacred space.[14] Space-making is often the first step toward community re-building. Many development ministries that succeed are careful with creating localized "sticky space" where people stabilize relationships. But at the same time, as explained in chapter 2, urban space disorients people, reshapes their self-identity, and diverts their desires. This presents challenges as well as opportunities for Christian outreach. After all, the Church is called to build communities of the excluded and outcast. Effective pastors and leaders need to understand how the migration experience fractures human identity and renders it fragile. When churches made up of urban professionals plan to reach out to rural migrants, they need to do so with pastoral sensitivity. On top of that, China's high surveillance poses more difficulties for NGOs or faith-based charity to secure urban space. More creative outreach strategies are called for. This will be my main topic of discussion in chapter 5.

---

13. Moltmann, *On Human Dignity*, 32.
14. Kotkin, *City*.

5

Good Samaritans

I was a stranger and you welcomed me.

—Matthew 25:35

Order your soul; reduce your wants; live in charity; associate in Christian community; obey the laws; trust in Providence.

—Saint Augustine

ONE OF CHINA'S BEST-KNOWN actresses, Li Yuan (forty-three), has left the screen at the height of her career to advocate for migrant workers who suffer from pneumoconiosis, an occupational lung disease caused by working in high-dust environments such as jewelry factories, construction sites and mines. People with this disease have particles of mineral dust built up in the lungs, making the organs harden and darken in color. Although the same disease has been eliminated in most western countries, it is estimated that over six million migrant workers in China suffer from this disease.[1] According to a survey by charity organization Love Save Pneumoconiosis (*da'aiqingchen*), only a quarter of victims bothered to seek compensation from either the government or their employer.[2]

Yuan confesses that her once-privileged life as a celebrity used to make her utterly indifferent to the suffering of the migrants. She

---

1. "Survey Details"; Xia et al., "Prevalence of Pneumoconiosis," 8612–21.
2. Xia et al., "Prevalence of Pneumoconiosis," 8612–21.

owned many pieces of brand-name jewelry and luxury purses, and she liked to boast about them. But after Yuan became a Christian, she started to see these people as equals. Once startled by seeing an X-ray picture of a migrant worker with pneumoconiosis, she could not wave the images away. Yuan conscientiously connected the plight of this group to the much-coveted life of urban consumers.

> This migrant worker has to go through a surgery to have his lungs opened and X-rayed, in order to get proof for compensation. How sad! . . . Later I started to learn that our mines, our jewelry and jade, and even stonecutting can cause this disease. They were not told to wear masks when working. Or they used masks that were not safe enough to keep them from the dusts. . . . So when we are enjoying the view of urban high-rises and tasting delicious lunchboxes, you have to know that many silent migrant workers worked behind this scene. They had to return to their villages, leaving us this beautiful view . . . China has a pyramid structure in society, with peasants at the bottom. It is true that we are standing on their bodies. I would not forget the peasants who built these high-rises, and I would not forget the peasants who built our subways.[3]

Since then, Yuan quit acting and spent six years helping migrant families affected by pneumoconiosis in rural China. For the first time in her life, she was confronted with the poverty and human cost behind urban luxury. She donated large sums of money to support victims of pneumoconiosis for treatments, including a few instances of lung transplants. Yuan started her own charity foundation and began to publicly share about the humanity she saw in this group: "When I visited these villages, I found people there to be beautiful. When I looked into one of them, I felt like his eyes were speaking to me. He was very good-looking. If he was born in the city, he would probably become an actor and have a different life."[4]

3. Yuan, "My Awakening and Redemption."
4. Yuan, "My Awakening and Redemption."

While assistance from outsiders may help alleviate poverty or emergency for a time, it is does not necessarily lead to community rebuilding. In fact, rural migrants are suspicious toward outsiders, including NGO workers who are there to help them with good will. To most rural migrants, the fact that an NGO is trying to help them at the organization's own expense is simply beyond their comprehension. There have rarely been any free services they can access in the city, and they are suspicious of the idea of "charity." Such distrust is often a self-protective reaction.

Actress Li Yuan's efforts to aid rural migrants are among the few Christian witnesses that gained publicity on China's state media. In most cases, churches and Christian NGOs serve in obscurity. Even charitable organizations without any religious background face harsh political restrictions. Some background information is needed here.

In China, by 2014, it was estimated that about 1.5 million unregistered NGOs were operating.[5] These organizations range from self-support groups for special needs children and migrant workers' legal aid to women's rights and house-church groups caring for the homeless. In China, civil associations that are independent of the government are not legally allowed. Due to this constraint, many NGOs either choose to find an umbrella government body with which to formally register, or they operate informally. Fearing a "peaceful revolution" by social associations with international connections, local governments monitor the activities of NGOs by instituting a model called "buying services."[6]

Although Christian churches in other countries often fill a role in providing social support to disadvantaged groups, in China's cities, church groups made up of urban professionals are socially segmented from rural migrant people groups. Unlike in the United States, where the urban poor usually congregate in inner-city neighborhoods, in China, the urban poor are constantly

---

5. "Enter the Chinese NGO," para. 3; Chen, "NGO Community"; Lawrence, "Lions in the Communist Den," 24–27.

6. Quoted in Teets and Jagusztyn, "Evolution of a Collaborative Governance."

pushed to the suburbs because evictions or demolitions of shanty buildings find support in the state land ownership. Rural migrant churches are often led by ministers who were sent from their rural hometown churches. In the 1990s, there was a short-lived Christian revival in many rural areas of the country. But with the mass exodus in the same period of time, rural churches have been left with only the young, the weak, and the elderly. Therefore, the gap between urban churches and rural churches has enlarged.

Reconciliation within the Church

The authors of *Our God is Undocumented* record a ministry effort in 2008–2009 when a group of interfaith leaders held a communion service at the United States/Mexico border fence. People reached through the fence from the Mexican side of the border to celebrate communion with Americans. Christian advocates of this liturgical practice believe that it serves as a way of restoring equality and dignity to members of lower social status in the context of church.

Abraham Kuyper also once stressed the symbolism of church communion services serving real life functions: "Just as rich and poor sit down with each other at the communion table, so also you feel for the poor man as for a member of the body, which is all that you are as well."[7] Indeed, deeper reflections on "community" leads to an engaged theology in ecclesiological and sacramental ways. First, the church is the prolongation of the *missio Dei*—that is, God's engagement with the human condition in terms of redemption as manifested in the life and teachings of Jesus Christ. So, the church exists to pour itself out in service to a world that God loves. Secondly, the sacraments are equalizers for members of the church, the underclass and the middle class, the stranger and the local.[8]

---

7. Kuyper, *Problem of Poverty*, 69.
8. Sheldrake, *Spiritual City*, 145.

Having visited many urban churches and a few rural migrant churches, I have not heard of similar practices in China's cities. I did once attend a combined Sunday worship service of two churches—one made up of middle-class entrepreneurs and professionals and the other mainly composed of rural migrants. Members of the first church drove to the suburbs and gathered with the second church inside a large work shed that could hold up to a hundred people. It was apparent to me that this was a first-time experience for many urban professionals too. The rural migrant church which was hosting this combined worship cordially received us as guests. Their preaching and worship had a livelier style, given the fact that a few ministers were of charismatic background. Although they did not have a communion service together, the migrant church did prepare a simple meal for us guests. We were also invited to visit some households after lunch.

Reconciliation is needed between the gaps in China's churches. Without the larger picture of how structural injustice has locked rural migrants into perpetual hardships, very few members of the urban church could come to the kind of realization that Li Yuan did. I believe that her compassion to reach out to rural migrants was partly out of guilt. Although some scholars refer to the *hukou* system as China's apartheid rule, its effects and degree of violence are probably not as brutal as things were in South Africa. But there is certainly systemic injustice done, with one group (urbanites) enjoying benefits at the cost of another group (people of rural *hukou* origin).

In 2010, when I was teaching at a state-run university in Shanghai, I worked on a collaborative survey project with another Christian economist, Feng, in the same city. The survey compared academic achievements of migrant children in migrant-only informal schools and public schools that receive migrant children. While we were discussing the significance of this study, I mentioned the theme of social justice. As a labor economist, Feng responded with perplexity: "What does justice have to do with this?" If even an educated urban Christian who specializes in migrant labor could not see how justice is related to this issue, I would not expect many members of the urban church to echo Li Yuan's sense of responsibility for the migrant poor in the city. Most middle-class urbanites are not aware that their newly-renovated apartments are built by rural migrants who were not paid their full wage. The wall of ignorance and indifference between classes of people adds to the alienation of rural migrants in the city.

In his unpublished essay "Behemoth," economic historian Karl Polanyi once expressed lament for the indifference among social scientists, especially liberal economists, who benefited most from promoting their theories at the expense of devastating others. He argued that so-called values-free principles of empirical research has led to the de-moralization of academic disciplines. China's urban poverty is not a neglected research topic in academia. But state censorship has made most research a barren effort to contribute anything to the betterment of the situation. Ethical discussions are avoided. Little did my economist friend know that the consistent exclusion of ethics from economic sciences in history once prepared the way for fascism in Europe. When social scientists do not think and theorize primarily as moral human beings, they resemble what C. S. Lewis called "men without chests." Their impersonal theories or models could only produce outcomes that dehumanize the actors involved, including themselves.

Reconciliation entails a complex balance between structural change and spiritual harmony. Even if policy changes could grant rural migrants equal rights, they cannot guarantee reconciliation. Its process is often long and arduous, with many reversals, as witnessed in post-apartheid South Africa. China will need decades to address its wounds of internal migration. The least we can do is to start asking questions: What exactly needs to be reconciled? What is "justice" in this situation? In what ways has the witness of the church fallen short?

Advocacy for Restorative Justice in Education

For years, I have done research and written extensively for Chinese media, mainly to raise public awareness of the structural inequality experienced by the second generation of rural migrants.[9] This has been a most difficult process. Like any kind of advocacy in China, there is often more inertia than progress because the effects of institutional injustice are cumulative and irreversible. At the time of my writing this book in 2017, the third generation of rural migrants continues to suffer perpetuating exclusion from the urban education system.

Zhang Qidong, age thirty-seven, Shanghai's first rural migrant to receive the Model Citizen award, became a celebrity after another honorable advancement into Communist Party membership. Having worked as a blue-collar technician for twenty-one years, in 2007, he was promoted to a well-paid senior position. But even for Zhang, the opportunity for equal education for his daughter is still a distant dream. Without permanent resident status in the city, Zhang faces the difficult decision of sending the child back to his rural hometown for schooling. By September of 2007, according to the Shanghai Education Bureau, over eighty thousand migrant students who are enrolled in junior middle schools are faced with the prospect of returning to their rural high schools for qualifying exams and further education. These children have fallen through the cracks of China's education system characterized by rural-urban distinction.

In 2017, most migrant schools in China's cities are still struggling on the verge of "illegality." Due to the substandard facilities and illegal status, many became targets of evictions and clean up campaigns. Even in public schools that partially integrate migrant children, explicit rules of segregation tend to endure. Some schools even enforce strict "codes" against social mixing.

Sociologists of education differentiate between the primary and secondary effects of social background on education attainments.[10] In the Chinese context, the former refers to the effects of minority status on attainment tests during compulsory education, and the latter refers to the rates of continuing education afterwards. In China, only residents with local *hukou* are allowed to

---

9. Ma, "Migrant Children"; Ma, "Human Capital or Human Dignity."
10. See Boudon, *Education, Opportunity, and Social Inequality*.

receive public education and take exams to continue with further education. This system of "exam closure" in the current education system results in truncating many migrant children's educational trajectory. Almost every child of rural migrant family background, at some point in life, experiences being left behind. In the end, the majority of them drop out to take up informal jobs, following their parents and grandparents' city-bound journey.

In the 2000s and 2010s, many small NGOs helping migrant children were founded. Compared to workers' rights, children's education is a less censored issue in China. Many local governments tend to show lenience toward volunteers who came to show love to the poor children of the city. By 2017, the scale of NGO development, especially those with foreign connections, has attracted cautious attention from the central government. Following Xi Jinping's statements against foreign influences, a new NGO law was put into effect mainly through police surveillance. This clampdown discouraged over 7000 foreign NGOs from continuing the work in China.[11] Here I introduce two informal organizations with which I became familiar.

A training camp for NGO volunteers in 2007
(photo taken by the author)

11. Wong, "Clampdown in China."

Sons of Nature

As a researcher using participant observation in a number of charitable organizations, I discovered that they are often a small group of dedicated people who work on community-building over a long period of time. Sons of Nature (SON) belongs to this category. Every year, a core leadership team of three recruits around five volunteers to organize a summer camp for approximately fifty migrant children in Miyun district of suburban Beijing. The founder, twenty-eight-year-old Lin, believes that crowded migrant neighborhoods in urban centers have deprived migrant children of exposure to nature. So its core curriculum is to expose children to the stillness and wonders of nature, as supplementary educational experiences to their formal education. After two weeks of camp activities, volunteers accompany these children back to their neighborhoods and conduct family visits. Many relationships between SON volunteers and migrant families have lasted for years. Based on the needs of some families, SON workers and volunteers then sought other resources of support for them. But over the years, the most serious disturbances to their ministry were mass forced evictions and mass return waves during seasons of economic downturn.

Reading Together

Reading Together was founded in 2007 to enrich the social life of left-behind children in rural areas. Through offering wholesome reading materials and library space, the founders of this project envisioned instilling in young leaders a sense of responsible citizenship which would later help the deprived countryside flourish. This organization assigned one staff person (manager) to every new library it set up in a rural location. This manager shouldered the main responsibility for maintaining the library and nurturing local contacts, especially with rural schools in the locality. But this goal proved too optimistic for the employee, who is parachuted to a rural setting which is neither convenient nor welcoming.

Initial enthusiasm for the vision gradually faded into day-to-day struggles with loneliness and purposelessness. Ten years later, this organization had grown quite prestigious but was then ordered by the government to stop its work. A long-term NGO worker Kong (thirty-five, female) shared her observations with me:

> It is hard for NGOs to develop in this current political environment. The programs we do seem to help promote the agenda of the Communist Party. The children are inside schools, and the schools are inside this communist education system. So, it is like you are trying to penetrate through thick walls in order for the effects of good programs to reach the children. Most charity workers felt powerless. With Xi Jinping's campaign for reviving traditional cultures, NGOs and their partnering schools had to comply and do things for the sake of formality. But it is this kind of formalism that chokes the NGO spirit.

Kong summarizes by commenting that "the government is simply too powerful, and almost to the point that it can make you and your program disappear without other people knowing about it." I have heard from many NGO workers that civil space in China has now been compressed to what it was like in the early 1980s.

Evangelical Outreach to Migrants in Factories

New Stream is a group of twenty performing artists who stage their shows inside factories in smaller cities near Shanghai and Guangzhou. Migrants and Christians themselves, these young artists adapt real life circumstances into stage dramas that have a gospel core. Most of them are in their early twenties, single and enthusiastic. The ministry was founded around 2000 with the support of migrant entrepreneurs in the Yangtze delta area. They recruit young believers recommended by rural church leaders. Most of these young people have already worked odd jobs or were factory workers in the city. Such is the usual trajectory of rural youth after they finish secondary education at age seventeen or eighteen. When interviewed by the two mentors of this ministry, Wan (fifty-eight, male, pseudonym) and Cheng (forty, male, pseudonym), they are presented with a job and a calling to serve their own kind. Wan invited a few professional dancers and musicians who are Christians to train New Stream students to sing and perform with exuberant emotions. They usually perform in factories owned by Christian entrepreneurs. Some of these factories have a hundred assembly line workers, while some have a few thousand. After the stage is set up in a main hall, workers are informed about a special night of entertainment. All songs and drama are relevant to the hopes and concerns of migrants. Seeing the replay of departure from their rural homes, halting remarks of love through phone conversations with their left-behind children, and annual reunions with family, many workers had tears running down their cheeks. At the end of the two-hour performance, a lead actor would end with a restatement of the gospel message and an altar call. The response was always heart-warming when workers stepped onto the stage to express their willingness to accept Jesus as their Savior. Then the factory owner would assign local Christian mentors to connect with them.

Wan and Cheng often discuss with their team the level of effectiveness of their outreach. Overwork in most factories has been a factor deterring workers' participation and later commitment to Bible study fellowships. Their performance and messages may strike a deep chord with the needs of these migrant workers and thus attract many, but the lack of sustained church life is linked to waning faith commitments over time . Seven years after their factory performance model, Wan and Cheng experimented with installing pastoral leadership within factories in which they have performed. Given the long hours of work, usually twelve hours a day and seven days a week, new converts have been reluctant to make time for these in-factory church meetings. I once suggested to Wan that maybe he could advise the factory owners to give workers a day off. As Christians themselves, Sabbath-keeping is something they should be doing. Wan replied sadly, "I have already tried, but a day off for workers would mean the loss of one seventh of revenue to them." At a few mission conferences attended by Christian entrepreneurs, I was also surprised that this issue is not discussed.

Rural migrant workers in factories are a highly mobile group. Even in-factory pastors find it hard to maintain long-term relationships with new converts. The converts are also getting younger, as more and more junior middle school students in rural areas drop out to find work in cities. To some fashionable young workers, the kind of performance by New Stream was too outdated. Their leisure time, if there is any, can be taken up by other programs on their smartphones or in nearby internet cafes. So, it is increasingly difficult to present the Christian gospel in a way that the migrants find relevant to their lives.

Does the Bible offer an urban theology? As I discussed in the introduction, migration and the city have always been integral to biblical themes. If we can embed our daily anxieties and frustrations in urban life back into biblical narratives, we could understand our circumstances with fresh eyes. I think an urban theology appropriate for effective preaching can begin with the following questions: What is the meaning of "city" according to Scripture? When does it symbolize rebellion, and when does it epitomizes righteousness? In today's world, how do cities define or challenge who we are? What role does urban consumerism play in your perception of life's purpose? What are the urban manifestations of worldliness that the Bible speaks against? What are the counterfeit gods around us? As Christians, how do we respond to the worldview of urban privilege? While each city is different, one may have a stronger element of folk religions, while another is dominated by a competitive culture of achievement. How can preaching be relevant to challenge prominent idols of a particular city?

The meaning of the city and moral implications for urban life are rarely visited in sermons in Chinese churches. The urban reality composes such a dominant part of their daily life, but it simultaneously remains removed from what is preached in the pulpits. As the author of *Urban Apologetics* say, "The gospel should meet people at the point of their deepest confusion and at the height of their loftiest ideals. What matters most is that we bring Christ into every moment of human history and every point of human concern."[12]

Aiding Migrant Neighborhoods in Cities

Next I include a few examples of less formal evangelistic outreach efforts to migrant neighborhoods. For example, Provision Team are a loosely gathered group of Christians from two rural migrant churches in suburban Shanghai. They actually never had a formal name, and I gave them this name just to help the narrative here. Every other week, they gather and pray together, and then they head out for some rural migrant families that are especially in need of care. They leave them with some food and cooking oil, and they pray for them. They are familiar with many family circumstances, but such connections are not regular because of demolition and mobility of migrants. Occasionally when they are able to have educated volunteers join them, Provision workers bring them into migrant children schools as guest speakers for teachers and parents there. A few years later, they used a two-bedroom apartment to start an unregistered preschool for rural migrant families. In this way, their contact with parents of migrant families stabilized. By requesting parent-teacher conferences with teachers, the ministry taught biblical parenting. The scale of outreach through this project, however, is limited to around fifteen families.

Another outreach known as Bible Sisters started informally as a small Bible study group between an American woman, Sue, and two of her part-time house-cleaning maids from rural Anhui. Sue is a missionary and her cover job in Shanghai was as a professional fitness trainer. Her first house-cleaning maid Zhang became a believer. Since then, Zhang has been bringing her friends to study the Bible with Sue, often in a nearby McDonald's restaurant. In five years, their group grew to around fourteen women, with another educated urbanite Wei as Sue's assistant. Wei entered inner city migrant communities and met more neighbors of her newly

---

12. Brooks, *Urban Apologetics*, 31.

converted friends. In this way, a second Bible study group met regularly in a migrant family's home. The part-time work schedule of these house-cleaning women allowed them more flexibility to meet together. They formed an organic self-support group to share each other's needs. Once when a teenage daughter of a sister went missing after an argument in the family, Wei and other friends went out to look for her. Every Christmas, Sue would rent a big hotel conference room for this timid group of sisters to meet Christians from other walks of life for a special gathering.

A third example of outreach to migrant communities is Compassion. This organization was founded by Christians to assist migrant families through the building of community centers. One would expect the physical location of a spacious community center in an area crowded with substandard housing units to be appealing. At least the weekly movie night and after-school programs for young children always had good turnout. But most other times, these centers stay unused. One founding member of Compassion had planned to make his dwelling in the same neighborhood, but his plan did not materialize. So, the ten full-time staff members worked in air-conditioned office buildings while entrusting most programs to volunteers, mostly college students. Long-term neighborly relationships are hard to build. To the migrant neighbors, therefore, the compound looked more like another urban office building. These places and programs, which were initially set up to reach the neighbors, gradually grew into rigid and inaccessible institutions. Despite this reality, the founders of Compassion received wide media publicity and later expanded community centers in other global cities in Asia. They became increasingly content with mere statistics of outreach. As this organization itself became a multi-tiered hierarchy in the charitable sector, its initial dream of community-building has vanished.

Theological Reflections: How to Do Good in the Midst of Social Evil?

When good Samaritans in today's China want to help with the plight of rural migrants, they face complex challenges. In most instances, they already have the financial resources, but the need before them remains demanding and highly complicated. How to restore community among migrants themselves is always the key problem. Given migrants' high mobility and distrust toward outsiders, it may take any social program years to take root, and even then it is always subject to transiency. Although they are approaching a group that needs external aid, good Samaritans still need to guard against cultivating dependency. As the well-known documentary *Poverty Inc.* reflects, poverty relief efforts may develop a culture of paternalism when charity leads to more disparity of rights.

Secondly, spiritual accountability among co-workers of charitable teams is crucial. They need to realize that by acting on plans to restore justice, they are combatting a systemic evil that is much bigger than themselves. This applies to all kinds of mission work. Missionaries who entered foreign lands on their own face tremendous difficulties if they went without spiritual accountability or mentorship. Many used correspondence to maintain such spiritual connections with other members of the body of Christ. In this respect, New Stream, among all the case studies I mentioned above, has the most healthy support system of continued mentorship.

Thirdly, once an organization is set up, it may take on a life of its own. As Max Weber's classic thesis of "iron cage" claims, individuals have the rationalistic tendency to create rules and systems, but such procedures and their outcomes may, in turn, trap them in systems based purely on effectiveness and efficiency. Many charitable organizations like Compassion have traveled this path. Its initial vision and mission was often admirable, but ironically, the later bureaucratic structures led them to a path of rigidity, devoid of human compassion.

A fourth challenge is the question of whether community-building without the ministry of God's Word as its center is meaningful. A few organizations entered migrant or rural neighborhoods without explicitly informing people that they are motivated by Christian love. Their outreach programs are mainly inspired by social problems instead without being rooted in Bible teachings. Some Christian staff members quit these teams because they worry that the work is only "social gospel." In China's political environment, many NGOs that were founded by Christians were later required to submit to a legal entity of the avowedly atheist political system. Thus, the oxymoronic word "GONGO (government NGOs) has been coined. The independence of China's grassroots NGOs has always been questionable.

As Alexis de Tocqueville argues in the *Memoir on Pauperism*, once Christian charity is co-opted by state institutions, it loses the essence of human connections and rootedness.[13] State bureaucracy takes it on and turns charitable services into impersonal exchanges. Another danger is locating charity efforts in specialized institutions. When needy individuals are grouped together and categorized by specific labels, these practices, although out of good will, may produce unintended consequences of heightening the vulnerability of these people. Here is the irony of thoughtless attempts at hospitality—it can easily mirror worldly social distinctions that separate people into groups that deserve hospitality and others that do not. As Christine Pohl claims, such categorizing practices can be "the most dangerous forms of nonrecognition."[14]

Lastly, most urban ministries that reach out to rural migrants need to grow in the area of genuine and sustained Christian hospitality. For now, acts of Christian hospitality are often observed in emergency situations. For example, after the large-scale eviction of rural migrants in Beijing in 2017, churches used social media to send out information about free shelter on the Internet. Christians gave free rides and housing units to accommodate those in need. Hospitality happened naturally because it is at the core of the Christian gospel. One could also say that it is a fundamental expression of the gospel. In the early Christian

13. Tocqueville, *Memoir on Pauperism*, 31.
14. Pohl, *Making Room*, 79.

communities, hospitality was listed as a qualification for leadership. This has been true in China too, when Christians had no public venues to worship. Those who opened up their homes to become worship venues, often at the expense of inviting political harassment, gained places of respect and leadership.

Given the normally anonymous and transient relationship in urban settings, genuine hospitality and fellowshipping by Christians becomes a subversive countercultural practice. It does not stay on the surface of making connections; it has at its core the desire to know the personalities of strangers. Truly getting to know someone defies the norm of anonymity. Investing and sharing time subverts the norm of transiency. A church that hastens activities and keeps things merely in motion loses its savory taste, just as salt can lose its flavor. A redeemed community ought to have the ease and liberality of time to listen, to know and to serve. The world, in contrast, is always in a hurry. Partly because it could not afford the time—society is dying. Christian hospitality is a resistance toward the hustling trend of this world. Helping migrants name their experiences of oppression and alienation is another key component of community-building. Urban-dwelling individuals often echo with similar experiences too, although their circumstances are different. By spending time together and recognizing strangers for who they are, Christian hospitality is a process of humanization which restores dignity. John Calvin, in his *Institutes of the Christian Religion*, explains how the image of God impels Christian hospitality to strangers:

> the Lord shows him to be one to whom he has designed to give the beauty of his image ... God has put him in his great benefits with which God has bound you to himself. Say that he does not deserve even your least effort for his sake; but the image of God, which commends him to you, is worthy of your giving yourself and all your possessions.[15]

---

15. Calvin, *Institutes*, 3.7.6.

Indeed, while different social systems sought for a common humanity by worldly means, only recognizing the image of God in every person truly binds us together, despite our wrongdoing or neediness. It is the root for mutual recognition and respect. It is the foundation of human dignity. Thus, genuine Christian hospitality recognizes both vulnerability and dignity. In the gospels, Jesus Christ identified with every stranger in Matthew 25:35. Genuine hospitality and table fellowship are also important equalizers of relationships in the church. Historically, meal-sharing at the same table served to recognize the equal worth and dignity of individuals. The spirit of generosity is cherished when Christians emphasized including not only the needy, but those who could not return the favor. This practice is also rooted in the core of the gospel, for God invites unworthy sinners to dine with his Son as one body. Hospitality represents resistance to many layers of worldly trends: materialism, elitism, achievement-culture, entitlement, fragmented humanity, social apathy, anonymity, hedonism, etc. Therefore, one cannot overemphasis the importance of genuine Christian hospitality, for it not only spreads the credibility of the gospel, it also transcends social distinctions of superiority and inferiority.

6

Conclusion: Hope for a City

> The reason there will be no change is because the people who stand to lose from change have all the power. And the people who stand to gain from change have none of the power.
>
> —MACHIAVELLI

> The earthly city glories in itself;
> the Heavenly City glories in the Lord.
>
> —SAINT AUGUSTINE

A NEW DOCUMENTARY, *Plastic China*, presents alarming images of health hazards that face rural migrants who lack both knowledge and safety protection. As the world's largest plastic waste importer, China leaves millions of tons of plastic recycling to the lowest stratum of its working force—rural migrants. In one single village of suburban Qingdao city, migrant workers from poorer inland parts of China earn meager wages at a few hundred household-recycling workshops run by local residents. Unschooled young children of these poor families are shown happily collecting dying fish in a nearby contaminated river for a family meal. This documentary presents poverty and injustice of the global economy in its rawest, most tragic form.[1] Although recently China began a ban on

---

1. Zhao, "China's Environmental Woes."

importing plastic waste,[2] it will remain a difficult problem because of other health hazards risking the lives of poor migrants.

Christian ethicist Miroslav Volf claims that economic systems should be judged by three normative principles that are based on the doctrine of creation: freedom of individuals, satisfaction of the basic needs of all people, and protection of nature from irreparable damage.[3] We ought to lament that today's global economy has developed in opposition to these essential principles. As Volf says, "in contemporary technological civilization, which can boast of remarkable labor-saving innovations, human beings paradoxically work more than they have ever worked before!"[4] What's more, Global solutions to locally produced problems often have unintended consequences. As British sociologist Zygmunt Bauman says, "the global spread of modern forms of life let loose and set in motion enormous and constantly swelling quantities of human beings bereaved of their heretofore adequate ways and means of survival in both the biological and social/cultural sense of that nation."[5]

The System: Globalized Exclusion

Harvey Cox comments in the beginning of his classic work *The Secular City* that "if secularization designates the content of man's coming of age, urbanization describes the context in which it is occurring."[6] Max Weber referred to ancient China as an empire without "true cities" because they were not governed by local citizens (see chapter 3 for a discussion of this topic).[7]

---

2. Laville, "Chinese Ban on Plastic Waste."
3. Volf, *Work in the Spirit*, 15.
4. Volf, *Work in the Spirit*, 135.
5. Bauman, *Work, Consumerism*, 93.
6. Cox, *Secular City*, 3.
7. Weber, *City*.

CONCLUSION: HOPE FOR A CITY

China's urban planners favor "totality" and "gigantism" in their ways of reorganizing urban space.[8] During times of international showcases, such as the 2008 Olympics in Beijing and the 2010 International Exposition in Shanghai, "beautification of the city" becomes another justification for demolition campaigns. But as noted by urban activist Jane Jacobs, rational planning violently disrupts the healthy spontaneous order of human communities.[9] With the land system still under public ownership, many Chinese cities are seeing demolition and reconstruction campaigns directed by a coalition between local officials and private developers to wipe out slum-like dwellings. In cities, gated commercial housing communities are encroaching on low-rise old town neighborhoods. The urban poor are being gradually pushed to the invisible verges of the suburbs.

Considering the world as a whole, this imposing urban social change presents an ironic and contradictory reality. On the one hand, it has integrated the most distant corners of this planet into its all-providing system; on the other hand, it has also excluded the majority of humans from sharing these advantages. As Harvey Cox explains, urban society presents symbols and powers that reshape the worldview of its residents, often in a more secular direction:

> The ways men live their common life affects mightily the ways they understand the meaning of that life, and vice versa. Villages and cities are laid out to reflect the pattern of the heavenly city, the abode of the gods. But once laid out, the pattern of the polis influences the way in which succeeding generations experience life and visualize the gods. Societies and the symbols by which those societies live influence each other. In our day the secular metropolis stands as both the pattern of our life together and the symbol of our view of the world.[10]

When work has a totalizing effect on people's social identity, it also leads to human crisis. Some symptoms are apparent, such as

---

8. Kostinskiy, "Post-Socialist Cities in Flux," 451.
9. Jacobs, *Life and Death*, 222.
10. Cox, *Secular City*, 1.

child labor, discrimination and exploitation. Others remain hidden but prevalent, such as what Volf terms as the "stupefyingly simple actions done with monotonous regularity" on assembly lines.[11] However, that "such work is an assault on human creativity and is dehumanizing"[12] is not widely recognized even by Christians. Christian entrepreneurs in Wenzhou were zealous to use their factories as sites of evangelism but at the same time denied workers the basic need of rest. In a country like China where labor laws are not enforced, rural migrant workers have fewer legal weapons to protect themselves. The sole focus on monetary gain internalizes overwork as something desirable, and workers often voluntarily deny the opportunities for rest. The suffering then becomes self-inflicted, just as depicted in the documentary *Plastic China*.

When comparing Mexico/United States immigrants with China's rural migrants, Roberts (2007) argues that in both cases, land arrangements are mechanisms for socially stratifying (im)migrants.[13] In both contexts, out-migrating peasants participate in seasonal flows of periodically returning to their home villages where cultivation of farmland offers a reservation wage. Circular migration patterns are also highly dependent on the oscillations of border control policies.

The Core: Alienation

In China, the state-owned land system, together with the remnants of the *hukou* system, locks rural migrants into a class of permanent transients in their own country. The dual forces of communist control on society and global consumerism have together produced an omnipresent propaganda machine that directs society toward mere materialistic and utilitarian goals. As Miroslav Volf says, "A centrally planned economy that allows only a marginal role for the market results in alienation in work and tyranny over

---

11. Volf, *Work in the Spirit*, 35, 39.
12. Volf, *Work in the Spirit*, 35, 39.
13. Roberts, "Changing Dynamics."

human needs, because the choices of the economic actors are severely limited by bureaucratic decisions the economic actors have virtually no control over."[14]

While global consumerism seems to provide limitless products for consumers to choose from, the larger reality of consumerism itself is predicated upon coercion. It becomes a game that everyone ought to participate in. The "market logic" then becomes binding to everyone in daily life.[15] In the illusion that we are free, we have already lost the true freedom to simply "be" human beings. The core of the problem is alienation. The dilemmas brought by globalization are still human problems. To answer them, one needs address the three most fundamental questions: Who are we? Who is God? What does it mean to be human before God?

Augustine applied the Christian doctrines of sin and alienation to political-economic ethics. He proposed that justice takes on three levels of meanings. First, it refers to a person's right standing before God. Augustine put it best in his famous statement, "Our hearts are restless until they rest in Thee." Second, it forms the habit of the soul, a human being's wholeness with oneself. Lastly, it entails the virtue of loving one's neighbor, which includes external attitudes and actions of compassion. It is an Augustinian conceptualization that justice begins from within the individual.[16] It is an internal order, which originates from the internal aspects of one's state of the soul, and then flows out to the external actions. To this I can also add the social actions of justice, defined as "how communities give people their due and coordinate our life together."[17]

Augustine also emphasized the social aspect of justice. As Aristotle had said previously, "justice is thought to be 'another's' good."[18] External justice becomes a quality of character and virtue that rightly treats another person. Augustine even called

14. Volf, *Work in the Spirit*, 18.
15. Delgado et al., *Augustine and Social Justice*, 76.
16. Augustine, *City of God*, 4, 37–68.
17. McCracken, *Christian Faith and Social Justice*, 3.
18. Aristotle, *Nicomachean Ethics*.

lack of charity to one's neighbor "criminal" and an assault against God.[19] God ordained that human solidarity embeds individuals into social structures of unity. Such embeddedness includes several dimensions—an individual's connectedness with God, with self, with others, and with the world. We are born with an innate desire to belong to something greater than ourselves, a greater being or solidarity. In J. H. Bavinck's missiology, this longing for solidarity with something transcendent is described as part of our "religious consciousness."[20]

Correspondingly, failure at the first three levels of justice, being reconciled to God, ourselves and our neighbors, leads to three manifestations of alienation: detachment in one's relationship with God, estrangement from one's own self, and isolation from other fellow human beings. Primarily, the very first step of alienation is a corruption of the *imago Dei*, the measure of one's true self, inside the soul. In any circumstance, alienation starts with a sense of exile from our true selves. The external environment only aggravates this sense of estrangement, particularly in a modern world of perpetual fragmentation and anxiety. Our senses are immediately captured by the corrupt signs of reality, which intensify the human struggle. Thus, the outer problem, although it sometimes triggers the inner problem, is not the real problem. A Marxist understanding adds another layer of alienation between the human being and his or her material world due to a capitalist system. Not acknowledging the effects of sin and the causal processes of internal alienation, Marx regarded external institutions of suppression as the problem. No matter what kind of economic system one is in, estrangement still happens from inside out, following the Augustinian order. When social sin is normalized into a dominant culture, it drags everyone into it through socialization, as Walter Wink says:

> We are dead insofar as we have been socialized into patterns of injustice. We died, bit by bit, as expectations foreign to our essence were forced upon us. We died as

19. Augustine, *Morals of the Catholic Church*, I.33, 73, 244.
20. Bolt et al., *J. H. Bavinck Reader*, 233.

we began to become complicit in our own alienation and that of others. We died as we grew to love our bondage, to rationalize, justify, and even champion it. . . . Those born to privilege and wealth may miss life by having been installed at the center of a universe revolving around their own desires. Others, born to merciless poverty and the contempt of the ruling class, may miss life by never feeling really human at all. If the advantaged must die to their egocentricity, the under-privileged must die to their hopelessness, fatalism, and acquiescence in their own despoiling.[21]

An Augustinian view of Christian theology requires the following remedy: the restoration of human beings as God's image-bearers. It presupposes that the right place of the human soul before God is the real source of change. So, it would be important to solve the problem of alienation in a society dominated by unjust structures by first restoring individual selves in the image of God. But Christians also ought to recognize that the restoration of all three levels of relationships, with God, ourselves, our neighbors and also our world, is also imperative. They make an organic whole, and none of them should be excluded in favor of the others. I say this to counter the prevalent posture of retreat among too many Chinese Christians who think that saving souls is the most important task.

A work culture is dehumanizing when labor is demeaning to the human spirit and deprives workers of freedom and creativity. Behind the workplace norms, there is a global chain of production that results in this dehumanizing culture. Frequently, the prices at which developing countries must export their commodities in order to import food and manufactured goods are determined by powerful developed countries. Economists use theories to justify such unequal exchanges. Professionals and popularizers of contemporary economics and international finance have the ability to bring the world into line with their theories, termed as the

---

21. Wink, *Engaging the Powers*, 157–58.

"performativity thesis."[22] They are often enmeshed in discussing and performing for efficiency, leaving fairness and justice aside. There are some exceptions, however, in world-renowned economists like Amartya Sen and Douglas North have paid attention to the structures of justice. Sen follows the political philosopher John Rawls in endorsing that justice ought to be the "first virtue of social institutions."[23] The topic of how global markets should be governed morally is a discussion about capitalism itself, but it remains uncharted water for most Christian theologians. Many believers tend to think that discussions along this line risk diluting faith to a "social gospel." But a wholistic understanding of the Christian gospel has social and even political implications because of Jesus Christ's Lordship over all creation.

The Remedy: Hopeful Remaking

My decade of research in China has zoomed in on a period when the plight of rural migrants was simultaneous with and yet far removed from the rapid growth of the church in China.[24] I struggle to offer any shining testimonies of justice, as Gary Haugen so beautifully does in his book *Good News and Injustice*. Most people I write about are still in bondage, although churches are reaching out to them on a small scale.[25] I have a fear that one day, the suffering of this massive population would descent even deeper for China. Even now, the needs are so overwhelming, and the help has been so scant. Despite the lingering sense of powerlessness, I remain determined to write down this history of injustice. In China, discussions among Christians about social injustice have been confined to only small circles. The indigenous church's understanding of mission seldom has social justice in its vocabulary, much less in publishing. Publishing something

22. Healy, "Performativity Networks," 175–205.

23. Rawls, *Theory of Justice*, 3.

24. Ma and Li, *Surviving the State*, xiii, 106; Ma and Li, "Remaking the Civic Space," 11–18.

25. Ma and Li, *Surviving the State*, 106–118.

like this book would be out of the question in China. So I write for readers who are likely part of the English-speaking world, far removed from this bleak story of Chinese rural migrants. My purpose has been to document, testify and advocate for the broad conviction that the Christian faith speaks to these stories with hope.

As German theologian and activist Dietrich Bonhoeffer says, in the face of exclusive policies by the state, Christians' response and duty, apart from challenging the legitimacy of such injustice, are "an unconditional obligation to the victims of any ordering of society, even if they do not belong to the Christian community."[26] We cannot bypass the suffering of our neighbors. Rather, we must enter into their experiences of violence, stigmatization and alienation. As Christians, we are to exemplify what is meant to be a true human community. As Walter winks puts it,

> We are not commissioned to create a new society; indeed, we are scarcely competent to do so. What the church can do best, though it does so all too seldom, is to delegitimate an unjust system and to create a spiritual counterclimate . . . We merely prepare the ground and sow; the seed grows of itself, night and day, until the harvest (Mark 4:26–29). And God will—this is our most profound conviction—bring the harvest.[27]

So, amid this gloomy picture of migrant poor in the grinding machinery of capitalism backed by a communist regime in today's urban China, we still have hope. This hope springs up from the deep conviction of God's kingdom yet to come when He will make all things new, even for the human city. As many theologians remind us, the city of God is the center of the new creation,[28] and today the church is called to be a sign of the hidden kingdom as well as an announcement of the kingdom to come.[29] As theologian Timothy Gorringe puts it so well, "The city is both Babylon, the

26. Zerner, "Church, State," 225.
27. Wink, *Engaging the Powers*, 165.
28. Moltmann, *Coming of God*, 5.
29. Ellul, *Meaning of the City*, 130.

place of alienation, exile, estrangement and violence, and Jerusalem, the place where God dwells, sets God's sign, and invites humankind to peace."[30] We have hope because the earthly city is not irrelevant in God's eternal plan. Its signs of suffering ought to drive us into eager expectation for the perfect city to come. Moreover, belief in the eschatological transformation of the world gives human work great significance since it bestows value on the results of work as "building materials" of the glorified world.[31] According to Moltmann, Christians' "ethics of hope" should be guided by "resistance and anticipation."[32]

> This ethic, then, is christologically founded, eschatologically oriented, and pneumatologically implemented . . . Though this world is not yet the kingdom of God, it is the battleground and the construction site for the kingdom, which comes on earth from God himself. We can already live now in the Spirit of this kingdom through new obedience and creative discipleship. But as long as the dead are dead and we cannot achieve justice, love remains fragmentary. All its works remain in need of redemption . . . God's presence encounters human persons in the concrete forms of their liberation from hunger, oppression, alienation, enmity, and despair. These forms of God's presence, however, point at the same time beyond themselves to a greater presence, and finally to that present in which "God will be all in all."[33]

The word "eschatology" literally means the last things, referring to the final destiny of human beings and their world. Urbanization is an eschatological trend, and due to the accumulative effects of human creativity in science and technology, human societies are not likely to reverse to a mainly agrarian mode. Since around 2008, globally speaking, the city now represents the dominant human mode of existence. At the same time, this eschatological trend also

---

30. Gorringe, *Theology of the Built Environment*, 140.
31. Volf, *Work in the Spirit*, 96.
32. Moltmann, *On Human Dignity*, 108.
33. Moltmann, *On Human Dignity*, 108, 111.

implies that any understanding of our existence cannot be reduced to the material level, for an eschatological view is inherently spiritual. It is because the conflicts are spiritual in nature that we witness the dual processes of decadence and flourishing, the decay of the human city and the church's eager waiting for the coming of God's city. Belief in the sovereignty of God ensures us that human history is unquestionably under God's control and direction. So, the history of urbanization is not to be condemned as evil or irrelevant. Augustine's classic distinction in *The City of God* between sacred and secular cities does not render human history or built environments meaningless. Augustine presents a central question: how should Christians serve God and serve others in the human city, given the fact that all human cities fall short of the ideal in relation to the true justice present in the heavenly city.

French sociologist and theologian Jacques Ellul returns to the Augustinian theme that the earthly city is characterized by "a passion for domination" or a desire for glory.[34] The urban center is certainly the epitome of human control and of rational planning, assisted by bureaucratic and technological sufficiency. It has an unabashed pride in being such a power house of human creativity. At the bottom of its pyramid of achievements lay anonymous, mobile and expendable human beings. Those at the bottom cry out at the accumulated systemic injustice of laws, cultures and norms. Therefore, Christian work and witness in the public realm is essential. As Philip Sheldrake says, "Christians have a stake in its social structures and cultural realities, alongside and with everyone else."[35]

In China, church-based apathy for social action against systemic evil has often been justified by two priorities. First, the narrow understanding that the main mission of the church is individual evangelism. Secondly, social advocacy may bring stronger persecution against the church. The second motivator is strengthened by the belief that Christians ought not "mess with politics." But as an urban apologist says, "Our lack of thoughtfulness on the

---

34. Augustine, *City of God*, 145.
35. Sheldrake, *Spiritual City*, 28.

practical needs of people's lives will call into question our credibility in their eyes. Their perception of our faith will be that it is insensitive and uncaring about the heartache that touches their lives because of their affliction."[36] Nicolas Wolterstorff once aptly stated that the misery of our world is the suffering of God. This perspective alerts Christians not to participate in victimizing the poor and the oppressed, because "to pursue justice is to relieve God's suffering."[37] He argues that churches often succumb to the same worldly values in pursuing increase in membership and programs, but "to be the church means to be for others, especially the neediest."[38] Therefore liberation theology has something to offer; its merit lies in its alertness to systemic evil and the biblical commitment to pursuing the shalom for the poor and oppressed. The author of *Good News about Injustice* forcefully challenges the church with the following words:

> But there is one thing we [Christians in the West] haven't learned to do, even though God's Word repeatedly calls us to the task. We haven't learned how to rescue the oppressed. For the child held in forced prostitution, for the prisoner illegally detained and tortured, for the widow robbed of her land, for the child sold into slavery, we have almost no vision of how God could use us to bring tangible rescue."[39]

In the Old Testament, God's prophets remind the Israelites that their past experience of liberation from slavery in Egypt ought to compel them to speak up and act when seeing injustice. Hence Jeremiah spoke to the Jehoiakim (Jer 22:13): "Woe to him who builds his house by unrighteousness and his upper rooms by injustice, who makes his neighbor serve him for nothing, and does not give him his wages." The hope of the prophets does not lie in the possibility of injustice righted in this world, but in the vision of a new shalom promised by God, as Isaiah prophesied on human

36. Brooks, *Urban Apologetics*, 138.
37. Wolterstorff, "Wounds of God," 16.
38. Gornik, *To Live in Peace*, iii.
39. Haugen, *Good News about Injustice*, 26.

dignity related to labor (Isa 65:21, 23): "They shall build houses and inhabit them; they shall also plant vineyards and eat their fruit . . . they shall not labor in vain."

Migration is an oozing wound of our time globally. This is true in contemporary Chinese society with its semi-marketized economy and its ever-present communist state. Thus, migration ought to become a new locus for theological reflection within the Chinese faith community. China's atheist and totalitarian regime has a built-in impulse to be the omnipresent and omnipotent ruler of its people. The language, cultural symbols and ideologies of its propaganda machine often help to legitimate unjust policies. Such a formidable foe poses a great challenge for Christians to nurture an awareness for seeking what is true and just.

We now live in an era of global Babels. Christian theology helps us realize that there is a spiritual battle going on behind the scenes. Without a theological understanding of what is required in the economy and politics to protect human dignity, even a fully informed remedy on the predicament of migrants cannot escape the singular dimension of materialism. Meanwhile, we need to ask deeper questions. Why do cities make humans vulnerable? How do cities tear us apart? How is Christ relevant in our urban centers? Does justice still matter for individuals enmeshed in hardened structures of discrimination and exclusion and who even internalize such indignity? These questions and the reflections in this volume serve as a starting point for future conversations.

Bibliography

Anderson, C. Arnold. "Food Rationing and Morale." *American Sociological Review* 8.1 (1943) 23–33.
Aristotle. *The Nicomachean Ethics*. Chicago: University of Chicago Press, 2012.
———. *Politics*. Book 1. Chicago: University of Chicago Press, 2013.
Augustine, Saint. *The City of God*. London: Penguin, 2004.
———. *Morals of the Catholic Church*. Volume I. Bibliothèque Augustinienne 1. Turnhout: Brepols, 1949.
Bauman, Zygmunt. *Community: Seeking Safety in an Insecure World*. Themes for the 21st Century. Malden, MA: Polity, 2001.
———. *Work, Consumerism and the New Poor*. Issues in Society. New York: Open University Press, 2005.
Berger, Peter L., and Thomas Luckmann. *The Social Construction of Reality: A Treatise in the Sociology of Knowledge*. New York: Doubleday, 1966.
Bolt, John, et al., eds. *The J. H. Bavinck Reader*. Grand Rapids: Eerdmans, 2013.
Boudon, Raymond. *Education, Opportunity, and Social Inequality*. New York: Wiley, 1974.
Bourdieu, Pierre. *Language and Symbolic Power*. Cambridge: Harvard University Press, 1991.
Brooks, Christoper W. *Urban Apologetics*. Grand Rapids: Kregel, 2014.
Calvin, John. *The Institutes of the Christian Religion*. Grand Rapids: Baker Academic, 1987.
Cai, Fang, and Dewen Wang. "Sustainability of China's Economic Growth and Labor Contribution." *Economic Research* 10 (1999) 62–68.
Caiman, Jonathan. "In Beijing, a Mass Eviction Leads to a Rare Public Display of Rage." *Los Angeles Times*, November 29, 2017. http://beta.latimes.com/world/asia/la-fg-china-evictions-20171130-story.html/.
Campanella, Thomas J. *The Concrete Dragon: China's Urban Revolution and What It Means for the World*. Princeton: Princeton Architectural Press, 2008.
Cavanaugh, William T. *Being Consumed: Economics and Christian Desire*. Grand Rapids: Eerdmans, 2008.
Chan, Kam Wing. *Cities with Invisible Walls: Reinterpreting Urbanization in Post-1949 China*. Hong Kong: Oxford University Press, 1994.

Chang, Hongxiao, et al. "Should Jobless Rural Migrants Stay or Return?" *Caijing Magazine*, February 9, 2009. http://magazine.caijing.com.cn/2009-01-17/110066604.html.

Chen, Jie. "The NGO Community in China." *China Perspectives* 68 (2006) 29–40. https://journals.openedition.org/chinaperspectives/3083.

Chen, Yingfang. *Life and Memory in Shanghai's Shanty Neighborhoods*. Shanghai: Shanghai Antique, 2006.

Chu, Rongwei, and Xiaodong Zhang, "Chinese Migrants' Consumption Market: Wealth from the Bottom of the Pyramid." *Economic Theory and Management* 7 (2011) 34–47.

Cohen, Myron L. "Cultural and Political Inventions in Modern China: The Case of the Chinese 'Peasant.'" *Daedalus* 122.2 (1993) 151–230.

Cosden, Darrel T. *A Theology of Work: Work and the New Creation*. Paternoster Theological Monographs. Eugene, OR: Wipf & Stock, 2004.

Cox, Harvey. *The Secular City: Secularization and Urbanization in Theological Perspective*. Princeton: Princeton University Press, 2013.

Delgado, Teresa, et al., eds. *Augustine and Social Justice*. Lanham, MD: Lexington, 2015.

"Do Not Fill in Wrong Information on Hukou." *People's Daily*, September 11, 1955.

Dou, Eva, and Dominique Fong. "Homeward Bound: Beijing Boots Migrant Workers to Trim Its Population." *Wall Street Journal*, November 29, 2017. https://www.wsj.com/articles/beijing-evictions-of-migrant-workers-sparks-outrage-1511962464.

Eastwood, Robert, and Michael Lipton. "Rural and Urban Income Inequality and Poverty: Does Convergence between Sectors Offset Divergence within Them?" In *Inequality, Growth and Poverty in an Era of Liberalization and Globalization*, edited by Giovanni Andrea Cornia, 112–41. New York: Oxford University Press, 2004.

Ellul, Jacques. *The Meaning of the City*. Translated by Dennis Pardee. 1970. Reprinted, Eugene, OR: Wipf & Stock, 2011.

"Enter the Chinese NGO." *Economist*, April 12, 2014. http://www.economist.com/news/leaders/21600683-communist-party-giving-more-freedom-revolutionary-idea-enter-chinese-ngo.

Fairbank, John. *The Great Chinese Revolution: 1800–1985*. New York: Harper & Row, 1986.

Fairbank, John, and Merle Goldman. *China: A New History*. Cambridge: Belknap, 2006.

Foucault, Michel. *Discipline and Punish: The Birth of the Prison*. Translated by Alan Sheridan. New York: Pantheon, 1977.

Friedmann, John. "Four Theses in the Study of China's Urbanization." *International Journal of Urban and Regional Research* 30.2 (2006) 440–50.

Gaulton, Richard. "Political Mobilization in Shanghai, 1949–1951." In *Shanghai: Revolution and Development in an Asian Metropolis*, edited by Christopher

Howe, 35–65. Contemporary China Institute Publications. Cambridge: Cambridge University Press, 1981.
Gornik, Mark R. *To Live in Peace: Biblical Faith and the Changing Inner City*. Grand Rapids: Eerdmans, 2002.
Gorringe, T. J. *A Theology of the Built Environment: Justice, Empowerment, Redemption*. Cambridge: Cambridge University Press, 2002.
Groody, Daniel G. *Globalization, Spirituality, and Justice: Navigating the Path to Peace*. Theology in Global Perspective Series. Maryknoll, NY: Orbis, 2015.
Groody, Daniel G., and Gioacchino Campese. *A Promised Land, A Perilous Journey: Theological Perspectives on Migration*. South Bend, IN: University of Notre Dame Press, 2008.
Haugen, Gary A. *Good News about Injustice: A Witness of Courage in a Hurting World*. Downers Grove, IL: InterVarsity, 2009.
Hayek, Friedrich. *The Constitution of Liberty*. Chicago: University of Chicago Press, 1960.
Healy, Kieran. "The Performativity Networks." *European Journal of Sociology* 56.2 (2015) 175–205.
Huang, Zhen, and Xigan Deng. "Rural-to-Urban Migrant Workers' Consumption Behavior and Self-Identification." *Jiangxi Journal of Social Sciences* 11 (2014).
Jacobs, Jane. *The Life and Death of Great American Cities*. New York: Vintage, 1961.
Jensen, David H. *Responsive Labor: A Theology of Work*. Louisville: Westminster John Knox, 2006.
Knight, John, et al. "The Rural-Urban Divide and the Evolution of Political Economy in China." In *Human Development in the Era of Globalization: Essays in Honor of Keith B. Griffin*, edited by James Boyce et al., 44–63. Northampton, MA: Elgar, 2006.
Kostinskiy, Grigoriy. "Post-Socialist Cities in Flux." In *The Handbook of Urban Studies*, edited by Ronan Paddison, 451–65. Thousand Oaks, CA: Sage, 2001.
Kotkin, Joel. *The City: A Global History*. New York: Modern Library, 2006.
Kuyper, Abraham. *The Problem of Poverty*. Edited by James W. Skillen. Sioux Centre, IA: Dordt College Press, 2011.
Laville, Sandra. "Chinese Ban on Plastic Waste Imports Could See UK Pollution Rise." *The Guardian*, December 7, 2017. https://www.theguardian.com/environment/2017/dec/07/chinese-ban-on-plastic-waste-imports-could-see-uk-pollution-rise.
Lawrence, Susan V. "The Lions in the Communist Den." *Far Eastern Economic Review* 22 (August 2002) 24–27.
Lee, Ching K. *Against the Law: Labor Protests in China's Rustbelt and Sunbelt*. Berkeley: University of California Press, 2007.
Liang, Zai. "The Age of Migration in China." *Population and Development Review* 27 (2001) 499–524.

Limin, Yu. *Factor Analysis of Rural-to-Urban Migrants' Consumption Behavior.* Beijing: Business and Management, 2013.

Lipton, M. *Why Poor People Stay Poor: Urban Bias in World Develop-ment.* London: Smith, 1976.

Lu, Shen, and Katie Hunt. "Photographer Captures Bizarre, Intimate Scenes of Chinese Factory Life." *CNN*, February 23, 2015. https://www.cnn.com/2015/02/23/asia/china-migrant-worker-photographer/index.html.

Ma, April. "China Raises a Generation of 'Left-Behind' Children." *CNN*, February 4, 2014. http://www.cnn.com/2014/02/04/world/asia/china-children-left-behind/index.html/.

Ma, Li. "Human Capital or Human Dignity." *Initium*, December 02, 2017. https://theinitium.com/article/20171202-notes-wheretogo/.

———. "Migrant Children Falling into Quicksand." *Financial Times* (in Chinese), September 20, 2017. http://www.ftchinese.com/story/001074370/.

Ma, Li, and Jin Li. *Surviving the State, Remaking the Church: A Sociological Portrait of Christians in Mainland China.* Eugene, OR: Pickwick Publications, 2017.

———. "Remaking the Civic Space: the Rise of Unregistered Protestantism and Civic Engagement in Urban China." In *Christianity in Chinese Public Life: Religion, Society, and the Rule of Law,* edited by Joel Carpenter and Kevin den Dulk, 11–28. Palgrave MacMillan, 2014.

Mann, Susan. "Urbanization and Historical Change in China." *Modern China* 10.1 (1984) 94.

McCracken, Vic, ed. *Christian Faith and Social Justice: Five Views.* New York: Bloomsbury Academic, 2014.

"Migrant Labor: The Internal Power of China's Reform." *Forum of Public Policy Reform and Service Innovation for Migrant Workers.* Paper presented at the *Nongminggong gonggong zhengce yu fuwu chuangxin* (Public Policy Reform and Service Innovation for Migrant Workers) Conference, organized by the NGO Beijing Facilitator, Peking, China, November 2004.

"Migrant Workers: Urban Underclass." *China Daily*, April 14, 2004. http://www.chinadaily.com.cn/english/doc/2004-04/14/content_323279.htm.

Mitchell, Tom. "Daunting Departure." *Financial Times*, January 7, 2009. https://www.ft.com/content/b3990974-dcf1-11dd-a2a9-000077b07658.

"Mobilize Nonproductive Individuals to Return in a Planned Way." *People's Daily*, August 16, 1957.

Moltmann, Jürgen. *The Coming of God: Christian Eschatology.* Translated by Margaret Kohl. Minneapolis: Fortress, 1996.

———. *On Human Dignity: Political Theology and Ethics.* Translated by M. Douglas Meeks. Minneapolis: Fortress, 1984.

Mote, Frederick W. "The City in Traditional Chinese Civilization." In *Traditional China,* edited by James T. C. Liu and Wei-Ming Tu, 48–49. Asian Civilization. Englewood Cliffs, NJ: Prentice Hall, 1970.

Myers, Ched, and Matthew Colwell. *Our God Is Undocumented: Biblical Faith and Immigrant Justice*. Maryknoll, NY: Orbis, 2012.
Niebuhr, Reinhold. *Moral Man and Immoral Society: A Study in Ethics and Politics*. New York: Scribner, 1932.
O'Keefe, Mark. *What Are They Saying about Social Sin?* Mahwah, NJ: Paulist, 1990.
Pohl, Christine D. *Making Room: Recovering Hospitality as a Christian Tradition*. Grand Rapids: Eerdmans, 1999.
Putnam, Robert. *Bowling Alone: The Collapse and Revival of American Community*. New York: Touchstone, 2001.
Rawls, John. *A Theory of Justice*. Cambridge: Harvard University Press, 1971.
Roberts, Kenneth. "The Changing Dynamics of Labour Migration in China and Mexico." In *Globalisation and Labour Mobility in China*, edited by Ingrid Nielsen et al., 200–201. Melbourne: Monash, 2007.
Scott, James. *Seeing Like a State: How Certain Schemes to Improve the Human Condition Have Failed*. New Haven: Yale University Press, 1997.
"Sexual Abuse of Children: A Horror Confronted." *Economist*, August 25, 2016. https://www.economist.com/news/china/21705848-china-has-millions-sexually-abused-children-it-beginning-acknowledge-their-suffering/.
"Shanghai 2000 Population Census." http://chinadataonline.org/member/censusnew/yearbook/Aayearbook.aspx?ybcode=26C309C036BCF9C98599F9146586D85F&key=en.
Sheldrake, Philip. *The Spiritual City: Theology, Spirituality, and the Urban*. Hoboken, NJ: Wiley-Blackwell, 2014.
Shukai, Zhao. "Criminality and the Policing of Migrant Workers." *The China Journal* 43 (2000) 101–10.
Skinner, G. William. *The City in Late Imperial China*. Stanford: Stanford University Press, 1977.
Solinger, Dorothy. "China's Urban Transients in the Transition from Socialism and the Collapse of the Communist 'Public Goods Regime.'" *Comparative Politics* 27.2 (1995) 127–46.
Sterba, James P. "A Great Leap Where?" *Wall Street Journal*, December 10, 1993.
"Survey Details the Hard Road Travelled by China's Victims of Pneumoconiosis." *China Labor Bulletin*, July 31, 2014. http://www.clb.org.hk/en/content/survey-details-hard-road-travelled-china%C3%A2%E2%82%AC%E2%84%A2s-victims-pneumoconiosis.
Teets, Jessica C., and Marta Jagusztyn. "The Evolution of a Collaborative Governance Model." In *NGO Governance and Management in China*, edited by Reza Hasmath and Jennifer Y. J. Hsu, 69–88. Routledge Studies on China in Transition 48. London: Routledge, 2016.
Thompson, E. P. *The Making of the English Working Class*. New York: Vintage, 1963.
Tocqueville, Alexis de. *Memoir on Pauperism*. Translated by Seymour Drescher. London: Civitas, 1997.

Unger, Jonathan. *The Transformation of Rural China*. Armonk, NY: Sharpe, 2002.

Volf, Miroslav. *Work in the Spirit: Toward a Theology of Work*. 1991. Reprint, Eugene, OR: Wipf & Stock, 2001.

Wang, Juliang. *Plastic China*. Documentary. Surrey, UK: Journeyman Pictures, 2016.

Weber, Max. *The City*. Translated and edited by Don Martinale and Gertrud Neuwich. New York: Free, 1958.

———. *Economy and Society*. Edited by Guenther Roth and Claus Wittich. Berkeley: University of California Press, 1978.

———. "Politics as Vocation." In *Max Weber: Essays in Sociology*, edited and translated by Hans Heinrich Gerth and C. Wright Mills, 77–128. New York: Oxford University Press, 1958.

"Why Have Prices Jumped for Beijing *Hukous*?" *China Newsweek*, May 17, 2008. http://politics.people.com.cn/GB/14562/7216309.html.

Wilson, William Julius. *When Work Disappears: The World of the New Urban Poor*. New York: Vintage, 1997.

Wink, Walter. *Engaging the Powers: Discernment and Resistance in a World of Domination*. Minneapolis: Fortress, 1992.

Witherington, Ben, III. *Work: A Kingdom Perspective on Labor*. Grand Rapids: Eerdmans, 2011.

Wolterstorff, Nicholas. "The Wounds of God: Calvin's Theology of Social Justice." In *Hearing the Call: Liturgy, Justice, Church, and Word*. Grand Rapids: Eerdmans, 2011.

Wong, Edward. "Clampdown in China Restricts 7000 Foreign Organizations." *New York Times*, April 28, 2016. https://www.nytimes.com/2016/04/29/world/asia/china-foreign-ngo-law.html.

Wu, Fulong. *China's Emerging Cities: The Making of New Urbanism*. London: Routledge, 2007.

Wu, Yuwen. "The Abuse of China's 'Left-Behind' Children." *BBC News*, August 12, 2013. http://www.bbc.com/news/world-asia-china-23628090/.

Xia, Ying et al. "Prevalence of Pneumoconiosis in Hubei, China from 2008 to 2013." *International Journal of Respiratory Public Health* 11.9 (2014) 8612–21.

Xiaochao, Li, ed. "China Statistical Yearbook 2008." http://www.stats.gov.cn/tjsj/ndsj/2008/indexeh.htm.

Yuan, Li. "My Awakening and Redemption." Public speech given at Fudan University, Shanghai, May 10, 2016.

Yusuf, Shahid, and Tony Saich, eds. *China Urbanizes: Consequences, Strategies, and Policies*. Directions in Development: Countries and Regions. Washington, DC: World Bank, 2009.

Zeng, Bijun, and Muxi Lin, eds. *New China Economic History*. Hong Kong: Economic Daily, 1990.

Zerner, Ruth. "Church, State, and the 'Jewish Question.'" In *The Cambridge Companion to Dietrich Bonhoeffer*, edited by John de Gruchy, 190–205.

Cambridge Companions to Religion. Cambridge: Cambridge University Press, 1999.

Zhan, Chengfu, and Xueju Li. *Grassroots Governance and Community Construction*. Beijing: China Social Science, 2009.

Zhang, Li. *Strangers in the City: Reconfigurations of Space, Power, and Social Networks within China's Floating Population*. Ithaca, NY: Cornell University Press, 1998.

Zhang, Lijia. "Factory Life Far From Home Leaves China's Migrant Workers Vulnerable." *CNN*, January 2, 2014. https://www.cnn.com/2014/01/02/world/asia/china-migrants-mental-health/index.html.

Zhao, Kiki. "China's Environmental Woes, in Films that Go Viral, Then Vanish." *New York Times*, April 28, 2017. https://www.nytimes.com/2017/04/28/world/asia/chinas-environmental-woes-in-films-that-go-viral-then-vanish.html.

Zhuang, Pinghui. "Evictions Waken Beijing Middle Class to Plight of Migrant Workers." *South China Morning Post*, November 30, 2017. http://www.scmp.com/news/china/policies-politics/article/2122124/evictions-waken-beijing-middle-class-plight-migrant/.

Index

Agricultural, nonagricultural, 12, 20–21, 24–26, 28, 34, 69, 79,
Alienation, 7, 10–11, 36, 44, 63, 65, 95, 102, 113, 118–21, 123–24
Augustine, 119, 120, 121, 125

Birthright, 20
Black market, 28
Bonhoeffer, Dietrich, 123

Calvin, John, 113
Capitalism, capitalist, 5, 7, 8, 13, 35, 36, 41, 61–64, 120, 122, 123,
Central planning, 11, 14, 19, 35, 61
Charity, 2, 7, 10, 96–99, 106, 111, 112, 120
Citizenship, 8, 13–15, 62, 65, 105
Civil society, 18
Collectivization, 12, 16, 22, 24, 36
Communes, 12, 21, 24, 27, 37, 93
Communism, communist, 2, 11, 12, 16, 18, 19, 21–23, 25, 31, 34, 35, 45, 62, 66, 99, 103, 106, 118, 123, 127
Consumerism, consumeristic, consumption, 11, 20, 50, 60, 64–66, 108, 118, 119
Cox, Harvey, 116, 117

Demolish, demolished, demolition, 2, 79, 80, 86, 100, 109, 117
de Tocqueville, Alexis, 7, 10, 112

Dignity, human dignity, 4, 5, 7, 10, 33, 34, 63, 66–68, 94, 100, 113, 114, 127
Discrimination, discriminatory, 6, 7, 33, 34, 38, 50, 51, 61, 73, 118, 127

Ellul, Jacques, 6, 8, 36, 63, 123, 125
Eschatology, eschatological, 8, 66, 94, 124, 125
Estrangement, 63, 120, 124
Exclusion, 7, 8, 13, 17, 31, 32, 63, 67, 72, 102, 103, 116, 127

Globalization, 7, 11, 64, 66, 119
Global capitalism, 8

Hospitality, 10, 112–14
Hukou, 14–17, 19–31, 34, 37–40, 48, 75, 77, 82, 86, 93, 101, 103, 118
Human capital, 11, 103

Ideology, ideological, 13, 18, 19, 21, 30, 41, 60
Image of God, *imago Dei*, 67, 94, 113, 114, 120, 121
Inherited status, 16, 19, 35
Institution, institutional, institutionalize, institutionalization, 7, 8, 10, 11, 13, 14, 17, 20, 29–35, 37, 61, 74, 103, 110, 112, 120, 122

137

INDEX

Justice, injustice, 4, 5, 9, 10, 11, 15, 17, 23, 30, 32–35, 38, 101–3, 111, 115, 119, 120, 122–26, 127

Left behind (children), 1, 104, 105, 107

Migrant communities, 3, 77, 94, 110

NGO, 3, 4, 6, 10, 11, 42, 55, 56, 73, 75, 84, 96, 99, 104, 106, 112

Olympics, 3, 4, 45, 117

Polanyi, Karl, 35, 102
Price mechanism, 31, 34
Price scissors, scissors' price, 20, 34

Rationing, 16, 17, 24
Relative deprivation, 50

Residence permit, 29, 80

Selfhood, 63, 94
Social identity, 81, 117
Social sin, 7, 10, 31, 33–35, 120
Sociology, 3–8
State media, 2, 3, 12, 55, 99
Suicide protesters, 2, 44

Urban poverty, 3, 6, 9, 66, 102
Urban economy, 2, 38, 56, 74
Urbanism, urbanization, 16, 25, 30, 31, 36, 44, 78, 116, 124, 125
Unemployment, 18, 25, 53–55, 62, 68, 75

Volf, Miroslav, 118, 119, 124

Weber, Max, 7, 17, 30, 32, 63, 111, 116
Wolterstorff, Nicolas, 126

Lightning Source UK Ltd.
Milton Keynes UK
UKHW021830030119
334926UK00005B/158/P